Praise from executives who know, live, and work with Gen Y's:

"*Plugged In* is thoughtful, practical, and so much more than a career guide—it's a life guide! It not only explains the forces that have shaped the lives of Gen Y's, but also shows them how to use their unique beliefs and values to find their place in the world of work."

—Tammy Johns, Senior Vice President of Global Workforce Strategy, Manpower Inc.

"*Plugged In* is a valuable resource for today's workforce. Tammy's observations and analysis will provide a foundation for the careers of the newest 'best and brightest'—and for their employers' global hiring strategies as well."

—Lisa Brummel, Senior Vice President, Human Resources, Microsoft

"Most organizations are still based on ideas and values the generation of Baby Boomers brought to work. This book will help the new generation entering work as well as their older bosses 'plug in' and find their way forward in the new organizational reality."

—Karsten Hetland, Vice President, Global HR, Nokia

"Gen Y's need to read this travel guide to the workplace before embarking on the journey of their careers. And for the Ys' managers, *Plugged In* is the most useful guidebook out there for understanding, getting along with, and productively employing members of the new generation."

—Steve Kerr, Senior Advisor, Goldman Sachs

"As *What Color is My Parachute?* illuminated the path for Boomers, Tammy Erickson's *Plugged In* provides the definitive guidebook to and for Gen Y. With practical flair, Tammy convincingly celebrates how the next 'greatest generation' will transform the way work works."

—Carolyn Buck Luce, Chair, Hidden Brain Drain Task Force

Gen Y Voices

"Erickson's approach is refreshingly constructive, making this book a great read for both Gen Y's and their colleagues. She has clearly taken the time to understand how my generation works, plays, and communicates."

—Silvia Gonzalez Killingsworth, Editorial Assistant, Condé Nast Portfolio

"*Plugged In* is an enlightening look at the events and situations that shaped many of Gen Y's thoughts, behaviors, and interactions. Tammy shows how our own unique perspective can be an asset, encouraging us to move ourselves forward and 'plug in' to the workplace."

—Robin Barton, Executive Rewards Team, Textron Inc.

"This book bridges generational gaps in the workplace. The author actually understands where we're coming from as Gen Y's and suggests effective ways we can capitalize on our expansive skills and strengths in order to succeed."

—Katie Miller, intern, Arizona Small Business Association, and student, Arizona State University

"*Plugged In* is a thorough and informative look at the actions and behaviors of Generation Y. It will be a valuable resource to managers, companies, and employees for years to come."

—Lindsey E. Heyle, Human Resource and Development Consultant, Assurant Employee Benefits

"An excellent book that all generations can understand, appreciate, and learn from! *Plugged In* articulates and applies what Gen Y's already feel but don't *know* about our generation, offering pragmatic insights that can be leveraged for success in a multigenerational workplace."

—Dawn Scarrow, Total Rewards Analyst, Yum! Brands, Inc.

plugged in

Also by Tamara Erickson

Third Generation R&D
(with Philip A. Roussel and Kamal N. Saad)

Workforce Crisis
(with Ken Dychtwald and Robert Morison)

Retire Retirement

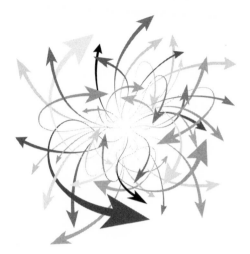

plugged in

THE **GENERATION Y**
GUIDE TO THRIVING AT WORK

tamara erickson

HARVARD BUSINESS PRESS

BOSTON, MASSACHUSETTS

Library of Congress Cataloging-in-Publication Data
Erickson, Tamara J., 1954–
   Plugged in : the Generation Y guide to thriving at work / Tamara Erickson.
        p.   cm.
   Includes bibliographical references and index.
   ISBN 978-1-4221-2060-6
   1. Generation Y--Employment. 2. Career development. I. Title.
   HF5381.E585 2008
   650.1—dc22

                                                                2008012892

to david and kate

the y's—and wherefores—of my life

contents

contents

part three
you got the job—now what?

acknowledgments

Writing translates into a lot of solitary time—and I deeply appreciate everyone who helped me through the process. Tom, most particularly, who keeps both family and farm well cared for when I am away or distracted. Sharon, who has done the same for our business over the past ten years. Max and the rest of the gang, who kept me company through the long weekend days.

The research for this book stretches back over five years of work and reflects the contributions of many colleagues. Bob Morison and Ken Dychtwald were lead partners in the original work. A terrific team worked on our most recent research, looking specifically at the needs and preferences of Generation Y: Espen Andersen, Tim Bevins, Anne Bishko, Laura Carrillo, Tim Donahue, Stephanne Ebsen, Maira Galins, Joe Grochowski, Barbara McGill, Bob Morison, Keri Pearlson, Margaret Schweer, and Sharon Randall. Special thanks to the companies that generously arranged focus groups for us with their Gen Y's: Arkema Inc.; The Home Depot, Inc.; Omaha Public Power District; S.C.

Johnson & Son, Inc.; Washington Mutual, Inc.; and Yum! Brands, Inc. Maggie Hentschel and Tim Bevins conducted research specifically for this book.

Matt Gregory, Cody O'Leary, Joe Grochowski, Mark Renella, JoAnn Heisen, and Ed Kamins read early versions of the manuscript; their thoughtful comments were greatly appreciated.

Many of the suggestions in the book are based on lessons I've learned from others. I extend particular thanks for the insights of Michael Carter, Lynda Gratton, Joseph Grenny, Sylvia Ann Hewlett, Herminia Ibarra, Blythe McGarvie, Paul Saffo, and Peter Scott-Morgan—as well as all those former bosses who have taught me to carry coffee and do the hula.

Steve Papermaster, CEO of nGenera, has created an exciting *next-generation enterprise* in which to work—one that generously supports the development of new intellectual capital. My colleagues, particularly Don Tapscott and Mike Dover, have shared their many insights and extensive research. Jacq Lewis, Mel Blake, and colleagues at Monitor Talent, and Danny Stern and colleagues at Stern & Associates, have been good friends and strong supporters throughout.

Warmest thanks go to the wonderful team at Harvard Business School Publishing. This book has benefited from the touch of multiple editors; I thank them all. At Harvard Business Press: Hollis Heimbouch, former associate publisher and editorial director, Jacqueline Murphy, senior editor, and Ania Wieckowski, editorial coordinator. Monica Jainschigg was invaluable in helping me create a coherent story. The HBSP community broadly has supported and engaged in this work: Angelia Herrin and Julie Devoll from its initiation; Paul Michelman and Jimmy Guterman as we explored the ideas further through HBSP Online, and Sherry Heffner and her creative team in HBSP Corporate Learning as we developed the ideas into learning tools. Special thanks to Carolyn Monaco, Michelle Morgan, and to Christine Turner-Vallecillo and Julie Devall, the ever-enthusiastic and supportive team in marketing.

Most important, thanks to all the Gen Y's who shared their views with me in our focus groups and in conversations over the past several years. Siamak Taghaddos, "Dan," Nate, and Allison Blood graciously shared the details of their personal stories. David's life provides many colorful lessons on a Gen Y's first experiences with work—all reflected with his consistently good humor. Kate's unvarnished and always useful advice sharpens my perspectives, and her enthusiastic support always makes me smile. Thank you all.

introduction

I suspect you already know this: you carry with you a wealth of talent, enthusiasm, and new ideas as you enter the workplace. As a Gen Y, the varied experiences you've had so far, your comfort with technology, the global and multicultural perspective that has permeated much of your education, the way you collaborate and communicate with your peers—all combine to provide you with strong work-related advantages. The truth is, without even trying, you will bring fresh perspectives to work because many of the ways you approach problems are different from the way "it has always been done." The world of work—whether in business, education, nonprofit, or government service—needs, and ultimately will welcome, the contributions you will make.

But chances are good that you will not find today's workplace immediately well matched to your preferences and style, and not quite ready to absorb all that you have to give. Much of this stems from generational gaps—different ways of viewing the world, and work in particular. Most organizations are still based on ideas and values that ran strong throughout your grandparents' generation. The role work plays in the lives of many older colleagues and bosses is probably different from the role you want it to play in yours—perhaps more all-consuming and financially motivated. Older bosses will often assume that you will respond to the incentives that motivated them at your age, when in fact such incentives hold far less appeal for you. The ways in which work gets done may seem counter to your natural instincts. The likelihood of misunderstanding is high, and the possibility that you may feel frustrated and boxed in is real. Without doubt, the way today's corporate world operates is not exactly the way you'd like to work.

The number of choices you face can also, for some of you, seem overwhelming at times. Unlimited options are not necessarily easy to navigate.[1] The decisions you face—about a career path, a place to live, a company, a role, compensation and benefit plans, additional education, life partners, and others—can be bewildering. It's not unusual to feel a sense of isolation and even sadness as you make these tough calls.

I hope this book will help you find your way forward—to create a work experience that is what you want. I hope it will help you not just survive, but thrive, through the choices you make. I know the world needs the energy you offer, the spark of new ideas you will bring. This book is about helping you plug in—connect effectively with diverse people of all ages and backgrounds and influence what's going on. It's about drawing insight from the world around you, at work and beyond— knowing what's going on. Plugging in means channeling your energy in ways that get your ideas heard and your plans put into action. For many of you who are already at work, this connection is something you may feel you are lacking in the workplace. This book will help you change that.

Although a lot of what you'll initially find at work may not suit you very well, you do have the opportunity to make significant changes. Sheer numbers are on your side. You are a large group, as big as—in the United States, even slightly bigger than—the Boomers, who have dominated U.S. culture for the past fifty years. Your generation will do the same going forward. Your tastes and preferences will influence not only available products and services but also the way things get done—the way work gets done. Your collective size ensures that you will have a significant voice in business and in the broader world.

Ironically, the numbers also work the other way in your favor. In some ways, your generation is not big enough. The economy has grown over the four decades since the Boomers first entered the workforce. Although you're a huge group, you're not big enough to take the places of the soon-to-be-retiring Boomers *and* provide much upside for growth. The economy needs each and every one of you. Most companies are beginning to be concerned about attracting and retaining talent. You will have the leverage to request arrangements that work best for you. You have the power to push for change.

You are Generation Y. You represent nearly a quarter of the world's population, and more than 20 percent—nearly 70 million strong—of all Americans living today. At such numbers, you will reshape the world, now and for decades to come.

And you have more than just numbers on your side. You also have time. Blessed with an astonishingly long life expectancy, you have a horizon that will allow you to develop multiple careers, make and lose fortunes, head in multiple directions, and start over many times—if you choose to do so.

For many of you, your ability and willingness to take risks will be strengthened by a safety net that previous generations have lacked. The strong relationships you have with your family, and particularly the confidence you have that your parents will be there for you in a pinch, allow you to view your career choices with a greater sense of experimentation than past generations have done.

Your connection with the forces that will reshape the ways we work over the coming decades is undeniable. You are the first generation to be plugged in to technology from birth, to be at home in the wired world, to be unafraid of the lightning-fast advances in communication. For you it's natural to have virtual relationships, participate in online communities, and explore ideas in a global context. Although the workplace you are entering is beginning to change—driven by new technologies, new economies, and forward-thinking colleagues, including those of you who have already arrived in the world of work—you will play an important part in propelling change forward. At the same time, these shifts are fundamentally recasting the options you face and increasing the number of choices you can make.

This book is about figuring out what you want from work. And it's about going after your choices in ways that are likely to be most effective—that will plug in to the people and practices you'll find in the workplace. It's about placing your commitment to work within the context of other priorities in your life.

For the past five years, I've been conducting research specifically on the changing role that work plays in people's lives and the reasons different generations often appear to think and act in conflicting ways. Much of my work has looked at how work and the workforce are changing. I have had the opportunity to talk with many of you, and the perspectives you've shared about your goals and preferences are reflected in this book. Your voices appear throughout. My colleagues and I have conducted large surveys and focus groups with Y's who have been in corporate environments for several years.[2] And I've had your help in shaping the conclusions from this research, through your comments during workshops and speeches and your thoughtful responses to my weekly blog.[3]

I have also worked with senior executives and major global corporations for thirty years, helping them improve their business strategies and operational approaches. I draw on this experience to discuss how organizations work, how they are evolving, and how you—Generation Y—can succeed in these environments. Some of what I share reflects a core set of skills and behaviors that are as essential today in the workplace as they have been throughout the past thirty or more years; others tap in to the new requirements of the evolving business world.

I also discuss the colleagues you'll meet in the workplace and explore why, at times, their approach or reactions may seem so different from what yours would be. I explain why you'll occasionally ask yourself, "*What* are they thinking?!" Your success will depend, in part, on understanding how other generations think and work—and how you can plug in to work effectively with them.

This is a book that is first and foremost for and about you, so I begin there. In part I, I look at the common characteristics of Generation Y, those that are likely to influence your career, and the perspectives—right and wrong—that other generations may have of you. My focus in this book is primarily on Western, college-educated Y's going into business or professional careers.[4] My intent is not to paint you all with too broad a brush or to minimize important elements of your individuality; in part II, I talk more about personal preferences and needs. But first, I share some important data and factual context about Generation Y.

To succeed in any work environment, it helps to understand all you can about who you are and how you are perceived—both the myths and the truths. Patterns often provide valuable insights, and to that end, looking at the shared experiences of your generation gives you a valuable starting point for your individual career considerations. What are you up against? I talk about how Gen Xers often see you, what you do that drives some Boomers crazy, and why your grandfather's corporation runs the way it does.

Most important, I talk about what has shaped your generation's unique perspectives—the lens through which many of you view the world. Drawing on my research into generational patterns and preferences, I trace the evolution and underlying rationale of assumptions you may hold today and examine how they are likely to affect the way you see your options and interact with others. I hope you'll find that this perspective will help you understand why the world looks the way it does to you and why it looks very different to many others: why, for example, older generations may currently view you primarily as high maintenance and overlook your high performance; why they often mistake your intent to live your life fully today for an impatience that you'll soon outgrow; or why some may view your close ties to your family as a lack of confidence rather than a strong foundation of values.

From that baseline, I turn to you as an individual. Part II is about your personal career strategy. A strategy is, in essence, a choice; determining a career strategy is about choosing a path and selecting where to invest your energy and time. The trick with any strategy is determining *how* to make the choices: what criteria to use in separating good ideas—the ones that are best for you—from all the rest.

The criteria that your parents might have used as they planned their careers are not likely to work well for you. Your immediate path is likely to seem less clear; you have many more options. Part of your strategy will almost certainly involve choosing the best *mix* of activities—commercial work, social change, family and friends—and determining what level of investment of your time and energy in each area will be right for you. In part, your thinking will need to be about drawing limits and setting priorities, deciding when enough is enough. You need new ways to think about work that are suited to your generation and this point in time.

In this second part of the book, I give you some frameworks and questions to consider as you look for the right career, to personalize the search to your needs. These approaches build on my research into why people who enjoy their work do so and reflect the needs of Generation Y in particular. The discussion is organized around six steps:

✓ **Find your passion:** Doing work that you love makes a huge difference in your life. Although it isn't always possible, you owe it to yourself to understand the type of work you would love and the clues you can use to seek it out.

✓ **Identify your preferences:** Your day-to-day enjoyment of work is affected by four key elements in the work environment, what I term content, compensation, connection, and communication. You'll explore the options available in each of these categories and learn how you can look for work that will be the best fit with your personal preferences.

✓ **Target your place:** Where are you most likely to find the work that matches your passions and preferences? Many of you are not planning a career within corporations—at least not in other people's corporations. Yours is a generation of entrepreneurs and independent adventurers. I discuss careers in a range of environments, including education, nonprofits, and entrepreneurial start-ups, as well as corporations, focusing on how each is changing.

✓ **Align the practical realities:** There are practical trade-offs you need to recognize and balance against your passion and preferences—what you are willing and able to invest in time, energy, and money as you pursue your goals. I discuss how to factor in these considerations, and I share examples of how other Y's are making choices.

✓ **Find the perfect job:** You know what you want; now, how can you find it? What has worked for others, and where are the pitfalls? I discuss the clues you should look for that are embedded in company characteristics, potential colleagues' comments, and proffered assignments, and I describe how to evaluate each one.

✓ **Leverage your advantages:** What do you bring to the table? I review the wonderful advantages your generation brings to the workplace and explain why I believe you will make an important contribution to any organization you join.

These six steps and the frameworks and questions that accompany them are designed to help you sort through your life choices—the options that are both desirable and possible, now and in the years ahead as you continue to make new choices.

Finally, in part III, I offer some approaches for success after you've landed the job—what I think you need to keep in mind in order to work effectively in a multigenerational environment. I look at the key skills, both hard and soft, that are critical for your generation's success at work.

Understanding how—and, most important, *why*—other generations think the way they do will help you anticipate how and when their views might conflict with yours. In chapter 10, I show you how this insight can help you plug in with older colleagues more effectively—for example, how appreciating an older boss's view of the typical situations you'll encounter in the workplace will help you position your ideas in ways that are more likely to be heard and accepted.

Your ability to get what you want in the workplace—to be persuasive and make the type of impact you hope to make—will also be enhanced by ten practical tips. These ten lessons, although in some ways timeless and broadly useful, are ones I've selected as particularly important for your generation. They either reinforce and capitalize on your generation's strengths or, in some cases, address some of your perceived weaknesses.

Chapter 11 tackles two indispensable skills for Gen Y's to relate to the language of business and how you express it:

✓ **Remember, I'm not a mind reader:** The necessity of clear communication

✓ **Reason, reason is my middle name:** The influence of financial logic

In chapter 12, I consider eight soft skills that round out the practices that will increase your connections in the workplace:

✓ **Think positively:** The power of optimism and confidence

✓ **Why not do it yourself?** The excitement of initiative

✓ **Make the most of it:** The ability to turn learning into luck

✓ **It has to work for the other guy:** The benefits of pragmatism

✓ **Walk fast, carry a stack of papers, and drink coffee:** The importance of being perceived as purposeful

✓ **Clear the air and move on:** The satisfaction of direct discussion—and letting go

✓ **Do the hula:** The role of grace under pressure

✓ **Keep three months' salary in the bank:** The freedom to walk away

Unlike many other authors, I have a point of view that is fundamentally optimistic. You are a terrific generation, with enormous potential for both personal happiness and positive contributions to the world. Of course there are challenges—but other authors cover these in depth. There are also great opportunities ahead.

I hope this book will help you find ways to work on the issues that you care deeply about. Just as you have the ability to influence the work world, you have the power to make a significant change in the broader world. Whether your concerns focus on corporate competitiveness, the environment, education, poverty, or any of the other serious issues facing us, your generation can help bring about important change. If you want fame and glory, I hope this book helps you find that, as well. More than anything else, I hope this book will help you find the life balance that you want and one that will work for you and your family. I hope it will help you get plugged in—to work that fits you, to valuable relationships with family and friends, to your sense of self in the world.

This is a book for you.

who are you, and what does that mean for your career?

The recruiting officer told me she was very careful about outlining the qualifications required for each posted position, and yet fully 50 percent of the Gen Y candidates who apply today do not have even *one* of the specified requirements.

"What are they thinking?" Her frustration with your generation was boiling over.

"Hmm . . . do you have any children?" I asked.

Instantly her mood shifted. "Oh, yes." Her pride was obvious.

"And did you offer them any advice? Perhaps something along the lines of, 'You can do anything you set your mind to'?"

"All the time," she sheepishly admitted.

"Well, these candidates' parents did, too—and they listened!"

. . . . .

The events of your childhood—what you saw and heard, particularly when you were teenagers—have played an important part in shaping who you are today. As in this story, your parents' deep conviction that their children can do amazing things is one important force; your generation is the product of the most child-centric child-rearing practices the world has yet known. But many other forces, good and bad, have shaped you as well: terrorism, the technology you use, global warming, generally strong economic trends, and more.

You are a member of what I am confident will prove to be a great generation. Most of you are jumping forward with confidence, self-esteem, and a desire to live life to the hilt. And looked at through the eyes and experiences of other generations, you sometimes drive older colleagues crazy. But if you get the chance, you are also showing how to make organizations a more humane place for everyone. I am convinced you're going to be a wonderful addition to the business community—a geyser of energy, creativity, and leadership potential at a time when these qualities are what most organizations seek.

You know yourself as an individual. My intent is not to minimize important elements of your individuality; in part II, I turn to personal preferences and needs. My goal in this first part of the book is to provide you with a context and evidence for why *you as a generation* are the way you are and behave in the ways you do. In the three chapters of part I, I share the context that has shaped Generation Ẏ and the meaning of your common characteristics in terms of your opportunities for and perspectives of work.

✓ **The outlines of your generation:** Your birth years, diverse racial and ethnic patterns, life expectancy, and educational patterns

✓ **The events and trends that have shaped you:** Influential events, the communication and technology environment you inhabit, and cultural trends and family ties

✓ **Shared views and common choices:** Your sense of self, commitment to community, social responsibility, spirituality, life expectations, and career expectations

1. the outlines of your generation

So, let's start with the facts. Who is Generation Y? For that matter, what do we mean by a "generation"?

A generation is a group of people who, based on their age, share a common location in history *and the experiences and mind-set that accompany it*. The shared experiences in history are key—and that's what I explore in these first three chapters. What do you all have in common? And what does your shared history tell us about your beliefs and behaviors?

Throughout this book, I'll define *Generation Y* as individuals born during the twenty years spanning from 1980 to about 2000. The precise boundaries of your generation are still being debated. Demographers typically watch the behavior of a generation; when the behavior changes substantially, a new generation is declared. Because the youngest of you are still pretty young, the end point for your generation remains unclear.

generation y

BORN: **1980 to probably about 2000**

TEENS: **1994 to 2013 or perhaps even 2018**

AGE IN 2008: **8–13 to 28 years old**

Based on previous patterns, your generation will probably span fifteen to twenty years, thus encompassing those born in 1995 and perhaps even 2000. The oldest among you have been teens since 1994.

Your generation has been called by many names. Three of the most common are the Millennial Generation, signifying that your developmental years spanned the turn of the century; the Net Generation, reflecting one important influence on your lives—the rapid evolution of digital technology; and the Echo Boom, because many of you are the children of Boomers (people born in the eighteen years—1946 through 1964—following World War II). These seem a bit one-dimensional to me—you are these things, but much more—so I'll use *Generation Y* (or Gen Y) throughout this book. One thing we do know about most of you is that you aren't keen on any labels, so bear with me on that.

In this chapter, I outline some basic facts that describe and define your generation:

✓ Your generation's size

✓ Racial and ethnic patterns

✓ Your life expectancy

✓ Your level of education

In each case, I ask you to consider how each of these facts—for example, being part of a large generation—has shaped your outlook on the world and your assumptions about your place in it. Although this book focuses on Y's in Western countries and many of my examples are drawn from the United States, I include global information where it shows important commonalities or distinctions among Y's around the globe. As you'll see, despite some important differences, you share a number of common characteristics shaped by your citizenship in a global, wired world.

your numbers

Wherever the line is drawn, you are a very large generation.

You are the largest consumer and employee group in history—representing more than one-third of the global population. In the United States, you are some 70 to 90 million strong, depending on where the boundaries are drawn, or roughly a quarter of the total population. You represent a slightly smaller proportion of the population in some other countries—for example, the "Echo Boom" was a bit more subdued in Western Europe—and a larger proportion in others.

The implication of your size as a generation is that you are unquestionably influential. You represent a huge market. The younger half of the generation in the United States alone—Gen Y's aged eight to twenty-one—spends $139 billion annually and exercises a major influence over spending by parents and peers on a wide range of purchases, from clothing to software to cell phones to cars.[1] You have been studied and marketed to almost since you were infants. You will shape global tastes and buying patterns for decades to come.

You also clearly represent a major, and growing, presence in the workforce. By 2010, your generation will represent a component of the U.S. workforce approximately equal in size to that of the Boomers (see figure 1-1). Based on your size, Y's will dominate the workforce for the next forty years and will be a significant presence for at least *sixty* or so! As I discuss further in chapter 9, this will give you a significant opportunity to influence the relationship between "employees" (if that even continues to be the relevant term for the relationship) and those who seek to have work done.

Around the world, your generation is significantly larger than the Boomer generation. In total, there are about 2.3 billion Y's, compared with 1.4 billion Boomers. However, owing to low birthrates in Europe and Japan, the percentage of Y's in developed countries will be much smaller than the percentage of Boomers in these same areas.

racial and ethnic patterns

In the United States, you are the most cross-culture, cross-creed, and cross-color generation in history. Some 61 percent of adult Gen Y's (eighteen to twenty-eight years old) are white, 15 percent are African American, 4 percent are Asian, and 17 percent are Hispanic. About one-third of children under eighteen are racial or ethnic minorities. Many Y's are the products of biracial and multicultural marriages.

FIGURE 1-1

Generational shifts in labor force composition

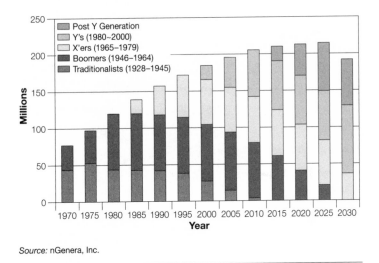

Source: nGenera, Inc.

You are as close to color-blind a generation as we've yet seen. For Y's, diversity, including acceptance of alternative lifestyles, is a fact of life. Six of ten teenagers today say they have friends of diverse racial backgrounds. Almost all (95 percent) of adult Gen Y's approve of blacks and whites dating, and 60 percent say they have dated someone of a different race.[2]

You are much more likely than older generations to see your-selves as citizens of a global world. Gen Y is coming of age at a time when the world is becoming less "West-centric" and when networks of individuals are becoming more influential than or-ganized nations. Most Y's, except those in Latin America, are more likely than previous generations to support globalization. Almost half—43 percent—of young adults between eighteen and twenty-nine in North America feel good about the fact that the world is becoming more connected through greater economic trade and faster communication.

Around the globe you are less likely than older generations to hold a sense of cultural superiority. In the United States, only 40 percent of those between eighteen and twenty-nine agree with the statement, "Our people are not perfect but our culture is superior," compared with 71 percent of those aged fifty to sixty-four.[3]

Encouraged by the Internet, the English language continues its dominance over other languages. Today there are 380 million native English speakers, another 600 million for whom English is a second language, and another 1 billion who are actively studying to learn the language. Interestingly, Y's hold varying views about whether English is a "must-learn" language for success in a global world; Y's in Eastern Europe are much more likely to believe that than previous generations in those countries did, but Y's in non-English-speaking countries in Western Europe believe it is less important than their parents did.[4]

Where does this leave us? Most of you have grown up feeling connected to some extent to a global community, and as a result, you have developed a strong sense of acceptance and inclusion. For many of you, this is reflected in your preferences about where you'd like to work and live. In the United States, many Y's are gravitating to communities that have significant ethnic variety. For most of you, being in a work environment that reflects racial, gender, and lifestyle acceptance is important.

life expectancy

You have remarkable longevity. Life expectancies have shot up over the past century, almost doubling in most countries. Most of you will probably have something like *sixty to eighty years* of healthy, active *adult* life—time to build multiple careers, work in corporations, try something entrepreneurial, return to school, invest in your family, and give back to making the world a better place.

Thanks to breakthroughs in health care and other quality-of-life advances, people are living much longer. From 2010 on, the anti-aging technology already available, such as cancer treatments, could increase life spans by one year *every* year. By 2030, the average life expectancy in most industrial nations will likely be one hundred, if all the available technology is applied. Some gerontologists believe that many of you will have life spans of more than 120 years.[5]

In the United States, average life expectancy at the time of birth increased by an astounding twenty-eight years between 1900 and 2000—a more significant increase in one century than humans have experienced in all their time on earth. As figure 1-2 makes clear, human life expectancy remained fairly constant (at about thirty-five years) for nine hundred of the past one thousand years before jumping sharply upward in a hockey-stick curve at the beginning of the 1900s. People born at the turn of the twentieth century in the United States lived an average of forty-seven years. People born in 2003 on average could expect nearly seventy-eight years of life at the time of birth.[6] This is by no means confined to the United States. Similarly long—and in many instances, longer—life expectancies from birth are found in many other countries.

Moreover, by the time people make it to your age, past the dangers of childhood illness and accidents, the probability further increases that they will live a very long life—perhaps one hundred years or more.

FIGURE 1-2

The sudden boom in life expectancy in Western societies

Life expectancy at birth: 1000–2000

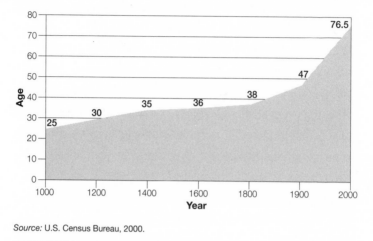

Source: U.S. Census Bureau, 2000.

As a consequence of longer life expectancies, all the milestones of life—and health—are shifting upward. When *is* middle age for you? The longer life expectancy most likely will *not* prolong your years of being "old"; for most people, it will extend the period of an active "middle." Much of this additional time will be spent in good—middle-aged—health. This is why I suggest that you think in terms of a career (or multiple careers) spanning sixty or so years. You will almost certainly live long enough that the idea of "retiring" into complete relaxation in your sixties will seem ridiculous.

This dramatic lengthening of life expectancy has already translated for many Y's into an unhurried life plan. You are already enjoying a prolonged period between adolescence and the settling-down stage traditionally marked by moving away

from home, becoming financially independent, getting married, and starting a family—in *New York Times* columnist David
Brooks's words, the *odyssey years*: "There used to be four common life phases: childhood, adolescence, adulthood and old age.
Now, there are at least six: childhood, adolescence, odyssey,
adulthood, active retirement and old age. Of the new ones, the
least understood is odyssey, the decade of wandering that frequently occurs between adolescence and adulthood." Others
refer to this phase as "emerging adulthood."[7]

In 1960, roughly 70 percent of all thirty-year-olds in the
United States had taken on these "adult" landmarks: marriage,
financial independence, and children. By 2000, only 40 percent
of thirty-year-old women, and slightly more than 20 percent of
thirty-year-old men, had done the same. Today, most Y's don't
reach these traditional adulthood markers until after age thirty.[8]

Even you hesitate to characterize yourself as an "adult." Only
40 percent of eighteen- to twenty-five-year-olds in the United
States, and only 70 percent of twenty-six- to thirty-five-year-
olds, answer an unambiguous "yes" when asked whether they
feel they have reached adulthood (see figure 1-3).

Reflecting this trend, the average age at which people get
married in the United States has increased markedly since 1970.
The median age for getting married is 28 for men and 26 for
women. Marriage occurs even later in Canada, where the average ages are 34 for men and 33 for women, and in Europe (37
for men in France, for example, and 29 for women; 33 for men
and 31 for women in Sweden, and 30 for men and 28 for
women in the United Kingdom). And the change in Europe has
been more significant. Between 1980 and 2000, the age of marriage has increased by six years in Germany and by more than

FIGURE 1-3

Do you feel that you have reached adulthood?

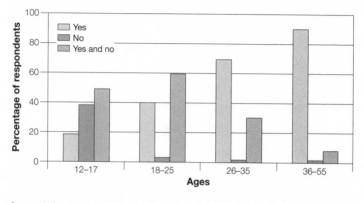

Source: Jeffrey Arnett, *Emerging Adulthood* (New York: Oxford University Press, 2004), 15.

five in the United Kingdom, for example, versus only slightly more than three years in the United States.[9]

Instead, as a generation, you are using your twenties as a time of exploration. You are staying in school longer. You are pursuing multiple interests instead of settling into "secure" jobs aimed at paying off mortgages. You feel free to do work—both paid and volunteer—that you love.[10] Most of you have no expectation that the first place you work will be at all related to your eventual career; your first job is not a "must-succeed." The implications of extended life expectancy are that many of you in the developed world feel a greater freedom to experiment and explore than previous generations did. You have time to make mistakes, to learn, to figure things out for yourself.

education

You are the most well-educated generation in history—but not by enough. The number of jobs that are designed for people with college or advanced degrees is growing faster than the number of you who attain this level of formal education. I discuss this gap—the mismatch between your levels of education and the needs of the evolving workforce—more in chapter 9.

Currently, only 26 percent of all thirty-year-olds in the United States have a college degree. As a generation, you are expected to do a bit better. Over the next decade perhaps as many as 30 percent of you will have a degree by age thirty, with more of you obtaining a degree later in life.

Are you surprised that the graduation rates are as low as they are? Does it seem as if almost everyone you know is going to college? In fact, many people *start* college. Two-thirds of twenty-five- to thirty-four-year-old high school graduates have attended some college. Some 46 percent of all eighteen- to twenty-five-year-olds are enrolled in school.[11] But only a quarter of you are finishing college—at least before you turn thirty—and that, as I discuss in chapter 9, is causing concern among employers about a future shortage of essential skills in the workforce.

To make matters worse, a significant number of you are not even getting high school degrees. The rate of high school graduation in the United States has declined to less than 80 percent, and in some parts of the country it is even lower. California's overall high school graduation rate is about 71 percent, and within that, the graduation rates for African American and Latino students are 57 percent and 60 percent, respectively. The

Los Angeles and Oakland unified school districts graduate *fewer than half* of their incoming freshmen within four years (although some people obtain General Educational Development, or GED, degrees later in life).[12]

It's not only the lack of degrees that fuels concerns about the skills gap. In a recent survey of executives and HR managers at four hundred companies, almost three out of four said recent four-year college graduates displayed only "adequate" professionalism and work ethic, creativity and innovation, and critical thinking and problem-solving skills. Only one in four rated graduates as "excellent" when it comes to the same set of skills. High school–only graduates fared worse: none of the respondents rated high school students excellent in any of ten qualities they thought important in a workforce.[13]

Whether or not the education you are getting or have received is perfectly suited to the workforce, there is little doubt that educational credentials shift the balance of power in the workplace. Two important trends affect your prospects: the educational shift between men and women in the United States, and the shift among countries in developed Western economies and the rapidly evolving emerging powers, particularly China and India. Let's look at the global situation first.

On average, Y's reared in the United States will not enjoy the same level of educational supremacy as did previous generations of Americans. Thirteen of the thirty countries that make up the Organisation for Economic Co-operation and Development (OECD) have higher graduation rates than the United States. Denmark, Finland, Germany, Ireland, Israel, Japan, South Korea, and Norway all have high school graduation rates of at least 90 percent, compared with less than 80 percent in the United States.

Other parts of the world are also rapidly increasing the educational credentials of their Y's, although perhaps not at quite the rate that some headlines imply. Although the raw numbers are staggering, many graduates in the emerging economies are hindered by educations that are not currently judged to meet global standards: "While these emerging markets are pumping out tens of thousands of graduates, only a small percentage of them are suitable for working at multinational corporations . . . You'll see that the schools in China and India are very focused on the theories and textbook learning," according to Anita Tang, a Hong Kong–based human resource (HR) consultant.[14]

India generates 2.5 million university graduates annually, of whom 400,000 are engineers and 200,000 are IT professionals. But even though graduates of the famous Indian Institutes of Technology and Indian Institutes of Management (IITs and IIMs) compete favorably with those from universities such as Harvard and MIT, the vast majority of the 11 million students in the 18,000 second-tier Indian colleges and universities are currently considered unemployable by top global and local companies. Despite these problems, India's Gen Y workforce is unquestionably much stronger than previous generations. The country possesses the highest potential among the rising economies for providing qualified young employees for global corporations and will be a strong draw for companies seeking to build or staff international operations.[15]

China faces similar challenges in producing graduates having the capabilities required for global firms. Fewer than 10 percent of the more than 3.1 million university graduates it produces per year are considered suitable for employment in a multinational company. And, as in India, Chinese students get little practical experience in hands-on projects, creativity, or teamwork, particularly in some disciplines, compared with their counterparts in Europe or North America.[16]

The third-most-attractive emerging supply of knowledge-worker talent is taking shape in South and Southeast Asian countries other than India and China. Together, these countries have a Gen Y population almost equal to that of either India or China, and more than one-third bigger than Eastern Europe and Latin America combined. Both the Philippines and Thailand, for example, have deep pools of university-educated young professionals.[17]

Within the United States, the educational patterns—and, many would argue, the accompanying balance of power between the sexes—are shifting, as well. Some 36 percent of female workers in their twenties in the United States now have a college degree, compared with 23 percent of male workers. Women now make up 58 percent of those enrolled in two- and four-year colleges. More than 50 percent of those enrolled in graduate school are women—and the gap is forecast to widen further.[18] This represents a significant difference between the generations. Among Boomers, a higher percentage of men hold advanced degrees (BA or higher) than women.

What does this say about the outlook for Y's as a whole? First, the educational shift between the sexes probably contributes to the delay in marriage. Educated women can get many of the things they want (income, status, identity) without marriage, and many find it harder (or, if they're working class, almost impossible) to find a suitably accomplished mate.[19]

The rise of a highly educated workforce around the world will certainly bring many new Y's into the global workforce, heightening competition for some of the best jobs. However, as I explain further in chapter 9, the anticipated demand for educated workers means that those of you with degrees have little to worry about, no matter where you live. There will be work for all of you.

If you haven't completed college, what about the future? What about *your* future? If you don't have it, should you get a degree? Is college essential?

At the risk of incurring the wrath of your parents, I'm going to hedge just a bit. Of course, higher education is a huge help (and given the current job market, if you can possibly get a degree, you should do it). But over the next decade, I suspect that greater opportunities will open in the United States to people with lower levels of formal education—more opportunities than have been available over the past decade. For example, several senior executives have told me that they are now hiring high school graduates who have strong technology skills for jobs that previously would have required college degrees in computer science. This is driven in part by the shortage of available college grads, and in part by a growing realization that many of the skills required for success in the new economy are not ones taught in school.

An excerpt from one of the most controversial blogs I've written outlines several arguments for the ways that the value of a college degree *might* change in the future.

from the blog files

questioning the future value of a college degree

Is it possible that the growing shortage of college-educated employees will actually, in an ironic way, *decrease* the value of a college education over the next several decades?

There are several arguments to be made on that side of the coin. One: as competition for college-educated employees increases, companies will become more and more motivated to use those without college degrees effectively in the workforce, in jobs that today would routinely require a diploma-in-hand as the price of admission. They will come to screen candidates in different ways—relying less on the stamp of a university and more on their own judgment of the individual's inherent capabilities and attitude—searching, perhaps, for those who are bright, motivated—and will make them money.

A second argument: in their desperate search for college talent, companies will join professional sports franchises in recruiting individuals earlier and earlier in the pipeline. It will become a sign of your exceptional talent to proclaim that you were hired in your junior or even sophomore year in college—only those in the lower ranks of the class will make it through as seniors.[20]

What's clear is that you, as a generation, are and need to be committed lifelong learners. Almost one-third—31 percent—of Y's rated the chance to learn new skills as a most important element of career development.[21] You like jumping in to new challenges and learning as you go. You apply for jobs for which others might view you as underqualified and relish the opportunity to "figure things out."

. . . . .

Your measurable demographics outline a generation that will play an influential role for decades to come. Your size has already prompted marketers—and, increasingly, corporations—to take notice of your preferences. Your long life expectancy gives you time to experiment and postpone some of the traditional adult commitments. You are well educated, generally accepting of others, and largely eager to join the economic scene.

But these numbers are not all that have shaped you. In the next chapter, I talk about some of the global events and cultural trends that have also influenced your development.

2. the events and trends that have shaped you

Do some of the older people around you seem to be operating under a different set of rules—or maybe even living on another planet?

In fact, they probably *do* have rules for life that are different from yours. Many of our most powerful impressions are formed when we are teenagers—when we emerge from our inwardly focused childhood and look out at the world around us. What we see at that particular moment in the world and in our families forms an indelible impression of how things work—and influences for life what we value, how we measure success, whom we trust, and the priorities we set. These teenage impressions shape our assumptions not only about the world, but also about the role of work within it.

It's logical that each generation forms its own unique impressions and therefore, to some extent, operates under a different set of rules: each group has experienced a very different world when they were teens. Your grandparents (or perhaps great-grandparents) came of age with D-day. Your parents had Woodstock. Neither of those generations had experiences that were remotely similar to each other, and both were very different from yours. These contrasts in the coming-of-age experience influence the generations' attitudes toward the world *and toward each other* for as long as they live.

This developmental model is based on the highly influential work on child development and learning done by Swiss biologist and psychologist Jean Piaget. Piaget concluded that children build cognitive structures—mental maps—to help make sense of their experiences. The time when most of us form our maps of abstract concepts and ideas is when we are teens. Thus the common teen experiences of each generation have a powerful influence on its members' shared beliefs and behaviors. Piaget also concluded that it is primarily *new* experiences that alter the developing child's cognitive structure rather than those that are perceived as having "always" been true.

In this chapter, I discuss the events and trends that may have seemed "new" to you when you were an early teen—things that almost certainly had a hand in shaping your mental models about how the world works. Of course, each of you has had slightly different experiences, depending on the country you were living in, your family's socioeconomic background, and a host of other factors. But as a generation, you also *shared* many prominent events, particularly in the era of global communication. It is this commonality of teenage experiences that gives your generation its shared characteristics.

The oldest Y's started to enter their teen years in 1994. The following experiences are likely to have been important influences on the conceptual models you developed:

✓ Witnessing significant global events, including incidents of terrorism, school violence, and natural disasters

✓ Experiencing the increasingly widespread technology and new forms of communication

✓ Immersion in a culture that included working mothers, increasing gender equality in many parts of the world, and a strong pro-child culture

Let's look at each one and explore how it may have influenced your generation's shared assumptions and common behaviors.

global events

Your generation has grown up under an unprecedented cloud of *random*, threatening events. Incidents of human-caused terror and natural disasters have made the world very unpredictable.

the world under threat

Inexplicable and unimaginable violence has been in the headlines throughout your teen years. Here are a few of these events:

✓ The truck bombing at the Alfred P. Murrah Federal Building in Oklahoma City that killed 168—April 19, 1995

✓ Bombing at the Olympics in Atlanta's Centennial Olympic Park—July 27, 1996

✓ Bombing of the U.S. embassy in Tanzania—August 12, 1998

✓ Terrorist attacks on the World Trade Center and the Pentagon that killed more than 3,000 people—September 11, 2001

✓ Ten separate bombings in the Madrid rail system, killing 190 and wounding 1,200—March 11, 2004

✓ A terrorist attack on London's public transportation system that killed 37 and wounded 700—July 7, 2005

And for many Y's, the incidents of violence in your schools—Columbine and Virginia Tech in the United States, Beslan in Russia, and, sadly, a number of others—have been even more visceral and therefore more significant than the other incidents in the formation of your mental models. Since 1996, there have been nearly fifty school shootings in the United States and at least ten worldwide.

Natural disasters, including Hurricane Katrina and the tsunami in the Indian Ocean that killed more than 225,000 people, have also been an increasingly prominent feature of your teen experience. Awareness of threats posed by global warming has increased around the world. Similarly, AIDS, BSE ("mad cow" disease), and the threat of Asian bird flu and other pandemics intensify for sensible teens the possibilities of a significant disaster in their lifetimes.

Your worldview reflects a high expectation of continued random disaster. Most Gen Y's (81 percent) expect another major terrorist attack to occur in the United States in their lifetimes. In 2005, 71 percent expected to see environmental damage from global warming.[1] I suspect the percentage would be much higher today. Almost anyone trying to make sense of things would conclude that terrible events can and do happen to anyone at any time; 87 percent of Y's believe that another natural disaster is somewhat or very likely.

The most common complaint I hear from employers regarding Y's is that you're too impatient; you want everything now. I believe that it is completely logical—inevitable, in fact, given the world you saw as teens—for individuals in their twenties to conclude that "living now" is a sensible thing to do. For many in Gen Y, living life to the fullest each day—now—is an important and understandable life priority. I believe that impatience—what I prefer to call your remarkable sense of *immediacy*—will be a lasting and perhaps the defining characteristic of your generation. You will not "outgrow" it.

activism: gen y's logical response

As teens, most of you have been highly sensitized to the issues facing people around the world—not only violence and disease but also the more insidious poverty and lack of education. Many Y's are moving to take direct action to address these concerns. You are the most socially conscious generation since the 1960s, and you are especially concerned about education, poverty, and the environment (see figure 2-1).

FIGURE 2-1

Top ten causes on Y's minds

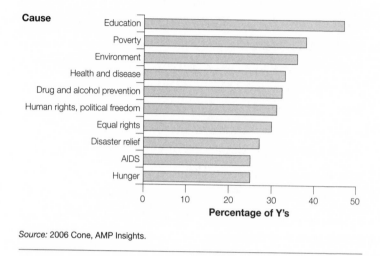

Source: 2006 Cone, AMP Insights.

Gen Y is leading a new wave of volunteerism, reminiscent of your Boomer parents' youthful passions. Today 61 percent of thirteen- to twenty-five-year-olds say they feel personally responsible for making a difference in the world. Eighty-one percent have volunteered in the past year; 69 percent consider a company's social and environmental commitment when deciding where to shop, and 83 percent trust a company more if it is socially or environmentally responsible. Two-thirds of college freshmen believe it's essential or very important to help others in difficulty, the highest level of social and civic responsibility among entering freshmen for twenty-five years.[2]

The approaches that you are using to tackle issues you care about are often hands-on and action-oriented. To begin with, you put your money where your mouth is. Boycotting is Generation Y's most popular form of civic protest, with 38 percent saying that they participated in a boycott within the past twelve months (see figure 2-2).

One-third of you say that you prefer brands that give back to the community, are environmentally safe, or are connected to a cause. One in four of you have purchased a product this year specifically because it was socially conscious. These and similar results suggest that you are the most socially conscious consumers to date.[3]

And, although the stories are anecdotal, many of you engage in a wide range of typically community-based, often globally linked initiatives:

FIGURE 2-2

Civic and political involvement of Y's

Percentage of young people who say they participated in these civic or political activities in the previous twelve months.

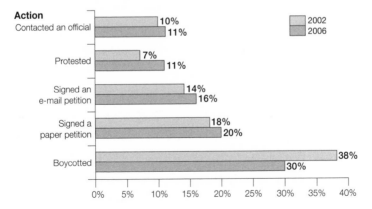

Margin of error ±2.6 percentage points

Source: Survey of 1,658 fifteen- to twenty-five-year-olds by Center for Information & Research on Civic Learning & Engagement, http://www.civicyouth.org.

> *[Stories of more than thirty young people in more than twenty countries who are taking action to contribute to their local and global communities] are stories of passionate, committed young leaders who chose not to look the other way when they saw a problem—the shame experienced by a person with HIV/AIDS, the poisoning of a sacred river, the frustration of a nation's citizens in the face of a national crisis, the exclusion of the physically disabled. These are young people who chose to take a stand . . . Youth are uniquely equipped to change the world because they dream. They choose not to accept what is, but to imagine what might be. Many . . . [young people] began their service work with little to no training, no money, and few connections to those who might help. Still, they persevered and successfully enrolled others in their efforts.*[4]

There is an important socioeconomic distinction in these trends in the United States: volunteering is class driven. In the words of Robert Putnam, Harvard professor of public policy, "This whole recent spurt is largely concentrated among kids of the upper middle class . . . The have-nots are actually more detached than before. I am hopeful that we may be on the cusp of a new more civically engaged America, but if that is all defined very sharply in terms of social class, then the news is not so good." And a report by the National Conference on Citizenship, based on nationally representative data from 1975 to 2004, echoes Putnam's concerns. It suggests the existence of a "large and growing civic divide between those with a college education and those without one."[5]

There is evidence that your generation is reversing the trend of Gen X'ers declining involvement in voting. As more members of Gen Y became eligible to vote, the trend in falling voter turnout among young people actually reversed in 2004 (when the oldest among you would have been twenty-four). In 2006, the percentage of individuals between the ages of eighteen and twenty-nine who voted (49 percent) represented an increase of nine percentage points from 2000. Although young people still lag behind older adults, the rise in voter turnout among those thirty and older was a much more modest three percentage points—from 65 percent to 68 percent.[6] You are the fastest-growing segment.

And you are spiritual; in most surveys, the number of Y's who say that they believe in God is higher than that of any other age group.[7]

ubiquitous technology

You are the first generation of unconsciously competent technology users. You gained your skill as naturally as you picked up your native language.

Most of you have had access to computers from your earliest days. Many of you do not even remember logging on to a computer for the first time; it occurred before conscious memory, when you were very young. "Today's kids," says Don Tapscott, author of *Growing Up Digital: The Rise of the Net Generation,* "are so bathed in bits that they think it's all part of the natural landscape. To them, the digital technology is no more intimidating than . . . a toaster." And, by the way, the next generation is following the trail you blazed: on a typical day, 83 percent of U.S. kids ages six months to six years spend almost *two hours* with some form of electronic media. Sixteen percent use computers, and 11 percent play video games.[8]

Your teen experience with technology has been light-years away from that of the Boomer generation, and even of Generation X. For a quick comparison and contrast of how different your world is from your parents', see "Technology—Then and Now."

Thanks to your generation's early immersion in the tech world, you are not threatened by its newness. You view computers

➤ technology—then and now

— Many of your parents took their college exams using slide rules (not quite the abacus, but close!). Handheld calculators were not widely available until most of the Boomers were through college.

— To run their first computer applications, Boomers stood in line to drop off stacks of punch cards for processing (and returned the next day to pick up the results, because the processing alone took hours). Almost all of you use computers comfortably and well, and you get instant answers.

— Older generations memorized information. You use search functions and, as a result, can focus more on skills related to finding, verifying, and applying information than on rote learning.

and communication technologies as an essential "good"—useful, efficient, and liberating.

the technologies you use

Limited only by your budgets, you adopt and abandon technologies as you—and the technologies—mature. In every case, you aim for greater speed and flexibility of interaction. For you, technology is all about efficiency. It's here to make your lives easier.

Does that sound like, "duh"?

This observation may seem obvious to you, but believe me, it's not obvious to everyone. In fact, I argue that it's a new

---

— Many of your parents (or grandparents) had party-line telephones when they were young; human operators and neighbors could listen in on their conversations. Calls were expensive and were made only in important situations. Today, almost all of you have personal cell phones and use them frequently.

— When your parents were children, physical space was the locus of information exchange. In our small town, my mother "ran to the store" three or four times every day—in theory to buy some forgotten item, but in reality to check on the latest events of the day. Now, Facebook and MySpace allow you to catch up on the news far more often without leaving the house.

— For Boomer children, electronic entertainment was broadcast media—centrally produced and passively consumed—but yours is active, ever-changing, interactive, and personal.

---

perspective when it comes to communication technology. How many of you have heard older adults—your parents, perhaps—lament that BlackBerrys and e-mail are ruining their lives? I have *never* heard a Y voice such a complaint.

You do not, by and large, let technology run your lives. Most of you are not stressed, for example, by feeling you must check e-mail regularly. Living with technology has taught you that not every communication needs to be dealt with—at least not within the same time frame. You have largely learned to manage technology, and its role in your life, in ways that are helpful and productive, not intrusive or anxiety-producing.

Many of you have clear protocols and explicit, simple rules, communicated among your friends, for technology use: use e-mail only if you must send a document (and don't expect a response); send a text message to coordinate or address an immediate need; share general information, updates, and photos on Facebook; and never leave a phone message (unless it's for someone's parent).

Growing up immersed in technology has shaped many of your assumptions and behaviors and has made activities that may seem odd to older generations natural for you. In chapter 9, I discuss how some of these natural-to-you, odd-to-others behaviors can give you a strong advantage in the workplace. Here, let's look at some of the technologies you use and see how different your usage patterns are from those of older generations.

CELL PHONE USE. You are the first generation to grow up with widespread ownership of mobile phones. Today, almost all of you—for example, 92 percent of U.S. college undergraduates—have personal cell phones. Twenty-five percent of eighteen- to twenty-four-year-olds, and 29 percent of twenty-five- to twenty-nine-year-olds, have *only* cell phones.[9]

TEXT MESSAGING. Those of you in your teens and early twenties are rapidly beginning to use cell phones primarily for texting, rather than voice-to-voice communication—a dramatic change in practice from those only a few years older than you. In the United States, those of you under twenty-five send three times as many text messages as those older than twenty-five. Eighty-five percent of college undergraduates have sent a text message in the past month (the average was 115 messages). About half of Y's surveyed say they have sent or received a text message over the phone within the past day, about double the proportion of those in Gen X. In Europe, the use of text messaging is even more prevalent. Many of you prefer texting even when voice communication is available. Gen Y users are showing a growing preference for semisynchronous writing instead of synchronous voice.[10]

By the way, there is evidence that your text messaging may be driving text messaging by older adults. The percentage of adults fifty-five and older who used text messaging doubled in 2006 to 20 percent; a principal reason was their need to communicate with their children. Almost one in three teens say they use text messaging to communicate with their parents.[11]

INTERNET USE. More than 90 percent of the Y's between eighteen and thirty in the United States, and 70 percent of the Y's between sixteen and twenty-four in major European countries, use the Internet regularly.[12] And there are more Internet users in Asia than in North America or Europe.

MOBILE ACCESS. Mobile access is growing rapidly among your generation although, relative to other areas of the world, Web users in North America are more likely to be tethered to their desktops. In one survey, only 13 percent of Y's in the United States reported having browsed the Internet from a mobile phone in the past month, compared with 76 percent in Japan, 60 percent in India, 44 percent in China, and 43 percent in the United Kingdom.

PURCHASES AND DOWNLOADING. You use the Internet for purchases and downloads. In the United States, 94 percent of you say you have bought something online, as do 96 percent in the United Kingdom, 97 percent in France, and 99 percent in Germany. Only 38 percent of you in the United States have *not* downloaded music or videos online.

CONTENT CREATION. One of the biggest differences in the way you use technology compared with other generations is your active participation in content creation. Many Gen Y's around the world create content, although the way you post content varies by country and region. In some parts of the world, such as Japan, blogging is the most popular approach. There are now more blog posts written in Japanese (37 percent) than in English (36 percent). In other parts of the world, including the United States and Canada, posting to personal Web pages or social networking sites is highly popular with Gen Y's; and in yet others, such as China, Y's favor participating in virtual communities. Whatever method is chosen, the propensity to create and be creative is deeply ingrained in Gen Y.

SOCIAL NETWORKING AND PERSONAL WEB SITES. Because of the influence of Facebook and MySpace, social networking sites have become part of the fabric of your lives in the United States and Canada. More than 50 percent of those of you under age twenty-five use social networking sites, compared with a bit more than 10 percent of those over twenty-five. The percentages are not quite as high in Europe, but the pattern is the same; younger Y's are the highest users.

Younger Y's—twelve- to seventeen-year-olds—are particularly involved. More than half of you (55 percent) say you use online social networking sites, and the same percentage has created online profiles. Nine out of ten of these younger teens use these pages to stay in touch with friends they see often; 82 percent use them to keep in contact with friends they rarely see in person.

THE METAVERSE. Not only are you communicating through technology, but also many of you are, in a very real sense, *living* parts of your lives in the virtual world. You are the most likely generation to be experimenting with life in a fully landscaped and populated online metaverse.

There is an interesting pattern of metaverse participation: highest among Gen Y's under twenty-five, negligible among older Gen Y's and younger Gen X'ers, and then popular again among older X'ers. It turns out that younger Y's are primarily playing massively multiplayer online role-playing games (MMORPGs) such as World of Warcraft, a game that has the look and feel of a Tolkien world or of Dungeons & Dragons. Players must collaborate, operating in guilds of apprentices, senior people, and journeymen who are masters of particular tools or weapons.

The older Gen X'ers are participating mainly in virtual communities, such as Second Life. Virtual communities are popular with Y's in other parts of the world: some 24 percent of you in China and 16 percent in India claim to have added or changed content on a virtual world Web site in the past month. However, this is clearly a niche activity in the United States (3 percent of Y's), Japan (4 percent), and the United Kingdom (4 percent).

Because MMORPGs are popular with many Y's, and because they are frequently misunderstood by older adults—most of whom view them as a waste of time—let me say a bit more about how they work. There is evidence that playing these games, and particularly playing them well, is indicative of highly developed leadership skills.

There was a time when computer games were primarily solo activities (remember Mario?)—one solitary individual trying to beat the system. But MMORPGs are communal activities, an elaborate form of collective problem solving, fundamentally social. Although the player is often physically alone, success is highly dependent on elaborate collaborative skills and the development of a reputation through individual profile and validation systems. For example, the secret to success in Warcraft is to recruit the right mix of talent to your guild. These games can increase problem-solving skills and creativity and are becoming a form of collaborative learning. Games reward leadership, persuasion, innovative problem solving, trial and error, and risk taking—all skills that will be valuable in the workplace.

the way you get things done

Your experience with technology has shaped a view that communication is ubiquitous—reaching everyone, at all times, with minimal cost. That view, in turn, has prompted you to create new ways of behaving and different approaches to getting things done. In chapter 9, I discuss the many advantages that your unconsciously competent use of technology will bring to the workplace. I'm convinced that you will help the old dogs in business learn a number of new tricks based on the ways you use technology—fast, asynchronously, spontaneously, collaboratively. And, not least, the unique role you've played as the technology authorities at home and in classrooms has left your parents and teachers in awe and has added to your sense of confidence.

In addition to these work-applicable skills, your use of technology is characterized by two other attributes: first, you blur the lines between work and play. You don't distinguish between being entertained, learning, and working. And you are changing our sense of acceptable time frames—and the definition of "urgent."

from the blog files

the new "urgent"

I got my first BlackBerry 5 or 6 years ago, when my son was still in high school. Needless to say, he was pretty impressed with mom's new, spiffy technology.

The day after it arrived, I left on a business trip to the West Coast. I was running a large meeting of senior executives, and felt very pleased when I coolly put my new BlackBerry beside my place—where I could glance at it from time to time.

who are you, and what does that mean for your career?

Soon the first message popped up. All caps: URGENT. CALL HOME.

As every parent knows, this is the sort of message that stops one's heart. I quickly excused myself, stepped outside, and called home. My son answered.

"Hey, Mom—do you know—where are my corduroy pants?"

Here's the interesting thing about this story: different generations react to it in *very* different ways. Most Boomers are appalled (and pretty certain I must have strangled him as soon as I got home). But I've never told the story to anyone under thirty who had a reaction other than puzzlement: What's your point? Obviously the question *was* urgent. Why would anyone object to sending a message saying so?

cultural trends that have shaped you

Every generation is shaped by prevailing cultural assumptions. As you entered your teens, the trends that touched you most directly are those associated with the family—the prevalence of working mothers and pro-child theories of child rearing.

working mothers

Just as you have grown up with computers and the Internet, many of you have also grown up with mothers who worked outside the home. As I discuss further in chapter 10, Generation X lived through the societal change and upheaval of moms going off to work—but for nearly three-quarters of Generation Y, your mom has *always* been at work. From 1975 to 2000, the labor force participation of mothers with children under age eighteen climbed from 47 percent to 73 percent. It has declined slightly during this decade, to 71 percent by 2005.[13]

As a result, Generation Y's attitudes toward women working outside the home are both more relaxed and more choice-oriented than those of any earlier generation. A study of Yale undergraduates in 2005 found some of the best and brightest matter-of-factly discussing their plans to choose stay-at-home motherhood over a career. Other research found that 37 percent of professional women are leaving the workforce. Yes, many say they want to come back, but in fact fewer than half will ever return to full-time jobs.[14]

With the release of these findings, the ranks of older executive women expressed shock, awe, and horror. "Don't they appreciate the battles we fought? The corporate doors we broke down to open opportunities for women?"

Well, in fact, you don't.

And, in my view, that is a wonderful thing. Boomer women and their predecessors have bequeathed to you an incredible gift—the gift of taking for granted your ability to work outside the home. You don't wonder whether a woman can be the CEO of a major corporation; you know she can, and many are. You don't wonder whether a woman can be the head of state, an astronaut, secretary of state, or one of the richest and most powerful self-made individuals in America; you know women fill all these roles, and many more. And you certainly don't wonder whether a woman can work full-time and rear children; in all likelihood, your mom did.

And because you (women and men) are not supporting a cause or joining a fight, you are free to determine the life path that is best for you and your families. The need to prove the abilities of an entire gender does not rest on your shoulders.

As a result, many of you are considering options for structuring your families that your mothers may not have imagined. Many of you know firsthand what it is like to have both parents working. Your mothers tried to do it all, but they weren't always successful in your eyes. Many young women are expecting their careers to take second place to child rearing (see table 2-1). Over the next decade, many high-potential Gen Y women will enter the workforce but will choose to leave or become underemployed in order to maintain a balance between work and family.

Some people argue that we are witnessing a dramatic shift back to traditional gender roles. However, this is an oversimplified interpretation of this trend. Women are redrawing the boundary lines between work and home, demanding more flexible hours and greater family benefits, but, as I outline in chapter 1, from a greater position of power than ever before. Given the overrepresentation of women in higher education and the growing

TABLE 2-1

Gen Y females feel a tug away from career as they age

Percent strongly or somewhat agree	Age 16–17	Age 18–20	Age 21–25
I would love to be a stay-at-home mom.	18%	30%	43%
My biggest fear is not being able to have a family.	14%	31%	39%
I want my husband to make more money than I do.	21%	23%	33%

n = 1007 females in U.S. and Canada

Source: Synovate Edge Study on Female Pressures, June 2006.

scarcity of top talent, women's departure from the workforce represents a huge threat—a major potential drain of talent.

As a result, companies that want to attract and retain this rich pool of talent are beginning to think creatively about how to foster work environments that provide compelling options for Gen Y women—and Gen Y men, many of whom also want more family time. Flexible arrangements, which I describe further in chapter 9, are part of the solution, but only a part. The issues run deeper; purpose and ways of relating are part of the mix.

Despite the attention placed on the progressive actions of some large companies, smaller employers are often leading the way toward greater workplace flexibility.[15] This is likely to steer more of you toward small companies than was true of past generations.

pro-child culture

From infancy, you have been immersed in a very pro-child culture—blessed with an almost cocoon-like level of attention from your parents and other adults. Over the decades since you were children, there has been a steady and impressive increase in the number of hours that mothers and fathers spend with their children each day. In addition, there has been a convergence in the way that time has been spent—more in activities that both parent and child enjoy doing together.[16]

There has been a noticeable shift in the overall philosophies of parenting. Your parents soaked up humanistic theories of childhood psychology and became increasingly involved in your lives. As a whole, Western society moved toward an authoritative rather than an authoritarian parenting style.[17] The movies adults watched when you were young depicted children as smart and adorable. Tastes in the mid-1980s shifted from the child-horror genre that had been popular for more than a decade—think *Rosemary's Baby* and *The Exorcist*—to films about wonderful babies and the adults who improved their lives by looking after them, including *Parenthood* and *Three Men and a Baby*. By your teen years, the frontier of reproductive medicine had turned to fertility, compared with the 1970s, when the focus was on contraception. Today, celebrities scour the world for babies to adopt. You have grown up in an era in which children are deeply desired.

The result is a generation of young adults who like and trust the older adults in their lives. Your generally positive experiences with adults as you matured have left you trusting of authority, much more so than X'ers or Boomers. Today's teens trust their parents (86 percent), teachers (86 percent), and the police (83 percent).[18]

Your generation is astonishingly family centered. As a generation, you have developed strong, positive relationships with your parents. Today, there is virtually no generation gap. Most Y's genuinely *like* their parents, sharing many common interests—including music, movies, and recreational activities—and even describing them as role models and heroes. Ninety percent of today's teens report being very close to their parents—a sharp contrast to the Boomers, more than 40 percent of whom said, in a 1974 survey, they'd be better off without any parents![19]

Most of you expect to retain close parental bonds even after leaving home. Roughly eight in ten of you who live away from home say you've talked to your parents in the past day. Nearly three in four see parents at least once a week, and half see their parents daily.[20]

One of the hottest trends in housing is the development of multigenerational complexes designed for Boomers and the budding families of their Gen X or Gen Y children. A number of you plan to go into business with your parents. Our research has shown that working at the same company as a parent is already a popular choice.[21]

Most members of Generation Y say they are likely to consult with their parents on all major decisions, including jobs. As one focus group participant put it, "I ask for advice on home buying, career paths . . . they're always looking one step ahead, and the advice is very valuable."[22]

There is, of course, the phenomenon called "boomerang kids." According to the 2000 U.S. Census, 4 million people between the ages of twenty-five and thirty-four in the United States live with their parents. To the astonishment of Boomers (remember, many of them thought they would be better off with no parents and left their childhood homes with rockets on their feet), plenty of college seniors say they expect to move back home after graduation. True to their word, 58 percent of college graduates between 2000 and 2006 did move home after school, and almost one-third remained there for more than a year.[23]

For many of you, the move back home is not a "failure to launch" but a natural, desirable extension of your relationship with your families. Many Generation X boomerangs tried to start independent lives but ended up moving back home when economic challenges or other struggles made it too difficult to go it alone. You are often motivated by other factors, including a genuine enjoyment of your parents' company, as well as a desire for time to rethink work. And you're pretty convinced that your parents feel the same way about spending time with you:

who are you, and what does that mean for your career?

"If we don't like a job, we quit, because the worst thing that can happen is that we move back home. There's no stigma, and many of us grew up with both parents working, so our moms would love nothing more than to cook our favorite meatloaf," says one Y. A recent survey reports that teens and young adults rank "spending time with family" as the one thing that makes them the most happy.[24]

But even though we hear a lot about boomerang kids today, the facts are not nearly as dramatic as the commentators make them seem. The percentage of Y's who live with one or more parents in their twenties is a bit higher than in previous generations—but not dramatically so (see figure 2-3).

Nor is the trend as pronounced in the United States as it is in many parts of the world. In France, for example, some 65 percent of people in their mid-twenties are still living with their parents—double the proportion who stayed in the nest in 1975.

FIGURE 2-3

Living with parents, by gender and age

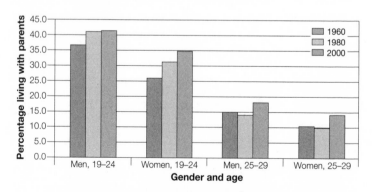

Source: Jordan Matsudaira, "Jobs, Wages, and Leaving the Nest," MacArthur Foundation. *Research Network on Transitions to Adulthood and Public Policy Brief* 35 (November 2006).

Many of you, on the other hand, have never even thought of leaving.

when does "our home" become "my house"?

I remember the day he said it for the first time. He had driven back to his apartment in Greenwich Village after having spent the weekend with us at the farm. When he called to let us know he'd arrived safely, our son said those fateful words that notched my heart as a parent: I'm *home*. In that moment, a cool jolt whooshed through some mysterious new space.

Despite this independence, it's clear he also continues to view the farm as "his" home. He returns whenever he needs a break from life in the city. He fills the old house with friends, who take over the kitchen and the grill—who make themselves at home. I have little doubt that he would feel welcome to return if times got tough.

It's easy for Boomers to judge this trend as evidence of a lack of ambition or competency on the part of their kids; but I disagree. I believe it is more properly viewed as a reflection of the close relationships Y's have with their families—and a changing cultural norm.

I was speaking with a group of business executives a few weeks ago, when one began to complain (good-humoredly) about his adult child's return to the nest.

"Hmm, I'm curious," I said. "When your children were teenagers, did you refer to the house as 'our home'?"

"Of course."

"And so, how did you communicate to them that 'our home' would revert to being 'your house' on their eighteenth birthdays?"

"Well, I certainly knew that when I was their age. I couldn't wait to get away."

My point exactly. They can wait. The idea that "our home" is always "ours" is becoming the norm.

Of course, an adult child lounging around in pajamas until noon is not a pretty picture. But the idea that "home" remains a place of safety and security is in my mind a good thing.

Don't judge Gen Y behavior by Boomer perspectives. And remember, Y's aren't mind readers. If you really want to tell them that their membership in the home ends at eighteen, I think you need to make that clear.

Personally, I am happy to renew the membership indefinitely.

There's a second named phenomenon evident in the parent-child relationship of Boomers and Y's: the "helicopter parent." Your parents' interest in your lives has not diminished as you have aged; some of them have gained this unflattering name because of their continued (and often inappropriate) hovering over your lives.

Some 60 to 70 percent of the parents of all college students are involved in some form of overprotective behavior. Most college-level helicoptering is done by mothers who are hyper-involved with their sons' lives; fathers are more likely to jump in periodically with strong-arm tactics to get results. Parents who hover too closely appear to cross racial and ethnic as well as socioeconomic lines.[25]

Colleges have been forced to respond. At the University of Vermont in Burlington, students serve as "parent bouncers" to keep parents from joining their children during student-only orientation sessions; Northeastern University in Boston offers a seminar for parents titled "A Time of Holding On and a Time of Letting Go."

And some *businesses* now find they face the same kind of parental involvement in their children's work lives. In one recent survey, 32 percent of the companies responding had witnessed parental involvement of some kind. The kinds of involvement ranged from the extreme of parents attending job interviews (4 percent of all the companies experienced this) and advocating for raises or promotions (6 percent) to simply submitting resumes (31 percent) and obtaining information on a company (40 percent reported this). In a particularly egregious example, one mother left this message with a company executive who had declined to hire her son: "Please call me. I think you misunderstood my son's qualifications. You're really missing out on a kid who would make a direct, positive impact on your company."[26]

The percentages reporting parental involvement declined with company size, indicating that parents are taking a more active role with larger firms than smaller ones.[27]

I've spoken with dozens of executives who've experienced this type of parental involvement, and the reaction is almost always negative. (Not exclusively—I had one senior executive tell me he preferred candidates whose parents were actively involved. In his view, this signaled good family values. But he is—at least today—in the clear minority.) One recruiting officer spoke for many in saying that she has yet to hire *any* recent graduate whose parent accompanied the grad to an interview.[28]

The reason for these strong reactions is that, for most Boomer and Gen X bosses, such parental interventions trigger an impression that people in your generation are clingy, dependent, and unable to stand on their own. In truth, I don't believe these negative perceptions are fair, but they are something you need to be aware of as you enter the work world. Although some corporations and bosses are ready to welcome parents into the recruiting process, many are not, and none that I've met so far are happy to have parents stay involved after you accept the job—for example, commenting on performance reviews or salary increases.

. . . . .

The events and cultural trends that you experienced as teens have given you some shared characteristics as a generation: immediate, optimistic, collaborative, asynchronous, and family oriented. In the next chapter, I build on these characteristics by exploring how they play out in the world, from your sense of self to the world of work.

3. shared views and common choices

Have the shared experiences of your generation left you with similar views or inclined you toward common choices?

They have, to some extent, but it's not a tidy portrait. You're not an easy generation to pin down. In part, that's because you are so global; the cultures of your country and traditions of your family are varied. In part, it's because you have very different socioeconomic starting points. And in part it's because you're, well—you. One of your characteristics is a strong desire to cultivate and express your own individuality, to customize.

And even among your shared views there are important contradictions. As a generation you are both largely optimistic and significantly overwhelmed. You are ambitious and yet less interested in "responsibility" than any previous generation was at your age. You are impatient but taking a leisurely path through life. You work collaboratively but, at times, seem self-absorbed.

In this chapter, I review your generational characteristics—how you see yourselves, what you value, and what you want from work—trying to identify traits that seem to apply to many in Generation Y and that will almost certainly influence your career path and choices.

your sense of self

How do you see yourself?

The experiences of your youth have shaped, to some extent, a set of traits that characterize your generation.

confident . . . and unapologetic

Most of you are jumping into the world with confidence and have a high level of self-esteem. Gen Y's as a whole are more than willing to express their own ideas, bring new thinking to issues or problems, and critique the way things have always been done if they think they have a better way. As one of you expresses it, "I've come to realize that the most significant characteristic of the Gen Y bird is that we are unapologetic. From how we look, to how spoiled we are, to what we want—even demand—of work, we *do* think we are special. And what ultimately makes us different is our willingness to talk about it, without much shame and with the expectation that somebody—our parents, our friends, our managers—will help us figure it all out."[1]

This sense of confidence is by no means a Western characteristic of your generation. Gen Y's in India, for example, are waking up to the huge potential and opportunity they face.

They tend to be extremely confident, to the point that retention has become a major issue. Wages in that country are currently rising at 16 percent per year, and turnover can exceed 40 percent.[2]

immediate

You are impatient and eager to live life now.

There are those who think that this is something you will "grow out of"—that when you get older you'll be willing to defer gratification. Some people claim that your impatience is a holdover from a childhood in which many of you perhaps became accustomed to getting what you wanted when you wanted it—new toys or clothes.

I don't agree. I think your sense of immediacy will be a hallmark of your generation until the end of your days. You will not grow out of it, nor is it caused by a pampered childhood. The events you witnessed when you were impressionable teens— the sudden, devastating, and unpredictable world events outlined in chapter 2—have left you with an undeniable impression that tomorrow just might be too long to wait: "[You] just kind of realize you're at a great time in life and you should just enjoy it while you can, because you never know."[3]

optimistic

Despite the terrorism and environmental disasters that occurred during your teen years—or perhaps even in part because of the contrast between those tragic events and the life you now lead—as a generation, you have an optimistic outlook. Some 84 percent of eighteen- to twenty-five-year-olds in the United States report that their quality of life is good or excellent, and 93 percent are satisfied with their family lives. Three-fourths have high expectations for their lives five years out (compared with only 59 percent of those twenty-six and older); 45 percent expect the lives of their children to be better than their own.[4]

This sense of optimism will likely be reinforced by many of your experiences in the workplace. Whereas Gen X'ers ran up against a stagnant economy and a tight job market, Y's are likely to find ever-growing demand for their skills. In some fields, this demand is already allowing you to approach work almost as paid "volunteers"—joining an organization not because it's the only game in town but because you genuinely want to.

overwhelmed

Ironically, your immediacy and optimism have a dark lining. Your optimism creates high expectations: most of you envision your life as an adult as highly successful; many of you may have views that are unrealistic. Your "unlimited" choices can mean endless decisions. Many of you are feeling overwhelmed—really overwhelmed. In one survey, more than 60 percent of recent high school graduates said that they had experienced some of the symptoms doctors use to diagnose clinical depression (see "Are You Depressed?").[5]

You are transitioning from a world in which you were on a pretty clear path; you knew what classes to take and what was required to succeed. But the challenges you now face are numerous and complex: you're choosing a career, a city, a company, a role, colleagues, and, for some, a life partner. You're determining how to trade off multiple priorities: money, passions, and aspirations. You're planning how to get out of debt, buy a home, and maybe even plan for retirement in the face of a collapsing social welfare system. Given the number and com-

are you depressed?

The symptoms of depression include sadness, frequent crying, feelings of worthlessness, hopelessness, changes in appetite or sleeping habits, or general lack of motivation to do things you once enjoyed. If you are experiencing several of these symptoms, you are by no means alone, nor should you be surprised. By definition of where you are in your life, you inevitably face a number of major situational changes that can easily trigger depression. If you are experiencing even a couple of these symptoms, please reach out. Help is there.

plexity of new decisions you're facing, it's no surprise that some of you feel overwhelmed.

And then there's the issue of our pace of life. The number of Americans who say that they "always feel rushed" more than doubled between the mid-1960s and the mid-1990s, with people from the ages of twenty-five to thirty-four feeling most anxious about the great many things that need to be done. For older Y's in particular—those of you who have entered the workforce—it would not be surprising if you feel busier and more stressed than ever.

Overlying these situational factors is the reality that the onset of depressive disorders most commonly occurs in an individual's mid-twenties. Although depression is sometimes linked to family history or genetic tendencies, depressive episodes also result from situational stress.

Alarmingly, in the same survey cited earlier, only 7 percent of the students experiencing depression had sought help. Individuals in their twenties rarely seek treatment for psychological disorders, because they lack insurance, time, money, or information about options for getting help. This inability to reach out often increases their sense of isolation.[6]

narcissistic? really?

Your generation does have detractors. It's popular to point out that as children Y's often received trophies for simple participation, and extensive praise for almost any idea. Detractors criticize you as products of a misguided movement in parenting and education that was designed to buffer you from the negative effects of competition and build your self-esteem—an approach, they argue, that has filled you with false self-confidence. Some people claim that self-esteem without achievement to back it up has produced an unmotivated and self-aggrandizing generation. A few have even latched on to the label narcissistic—focused only on yourselves and incapable of acknowledging or appreciating others' points of view or circumstances. Ouch!

The most negative conclusions are based on an analysis of thirty years' worth of data from a standardized narcissistic personality inventory, in which respondents score themselves against statements such as, "I think I am a special person." Based on this approach, the average college student's score on the inventory was 30 percent higher in 2006 than in 1982.[7] However, I find it a bit melodramatic to jump from this analysis to the conclusion that you are narcissistic. Nor does it track with my actual experience of interacting with you.

Although there is a real difference between clinical narcissism and healthy self-esteem, the semantics with which we describe the difference are fairly slight and have almost certainly been influenced by the changing cultural context. Even the dictionary defines *narcissism*—OK, granted, the fourth definition—as "the attribute of the human psyche characterized by admiration of oneself but within normal limits."[8] And some of the descriptors include people who love themselves; are optimistic, achievers, self-promoting, self-assured, success driven, and ambitious; think they can charm anyone, think they are better-looking than most people (something that may or may not be true), believe that they are special, are more a leader than a follower, and so on. Sound familiar to anyone? I suspect many of you have been encouraged from your earliest years to feel that most of these characteristics, at least to some degree, are highly desirable.

Think of the U.S. Supreme Court's struggle to define *obscenity*—and the clear recognition that our shared definition is changing over time. What clearly would have been obscene in the 1950s would scarcely raise an eyebrow today. The same is likely true of the language used in the assessment of narcissism. Our cultural norms have shifted. The parenting messages you received throughout your adolescence would have influenced the way your generation answered the standardized inventory, altering the implications of the various descriptors.

For example, in 1982, saying that you were a "special person" would have been uncommon behavior. However, today, after a lifetime of eating off those darn red "You Are Special Today" plates, you would probably be a bit odd—or at least a slow learner—if you hadn't been conditioned to believe that the correct answer to the question of whether or not you are a special person is an unqualified yes. For you, given current ways we use this sort of language, this answer doesn't pack the same negative clinical punch that it did a quarter of a century ago.

The critics are also concerned that the culture of praise you experienced as a child will reach deeply into the work world, suggesting that Y's feel insecure if they're not complimented regularly. Bosses are being made to feel the need to lavish praise on young adults with the threat that they will wither under an unfamiliar compliment deficit.

I'll let one of your own rebut this last point. "Young workers today aren't all spoiled attaboy-addicts," says Ryan Paugh, twenty-three-year-old cofounder of EmployeeEvolution.com. Although he agrees that twentysomethings today may be hungrier for feed-back than previous generations were, he adds, "People think of praise in the coddling sense. But what we want is guidance and mentoring—and praise *when* [my emphasis] we're on track."[9]

proud of your diverse tastes and styles

Ironically, one of your most shared characteristics is your diversity of taste and individual preferences.

Yours is a world of proliferation—of brands, media, product types, and channels. Gone are the days when Boomers counted down the top ten hits; you compose iPod playlists chosen from millions of available tunes. Amazon.com gives you the choice of hundreds of thousands of books, both in and out of print. One search on the Internet will turn up hundreds of options for almost any electronic gadget you are looking to buy. Boomers may roll their eyes at the number of variations on coffee offered by Starbucks, but most of you like it that way.

You love exercising the freedom that comes with this range of options. Only 13 percent of you strongly agree with the statement, "There is so much to choose from that when I buy something, I tend to wonder if I have made the right decision." Most of you feel well informed and confident in your purchase decisions; 83 percent say you usually know what you want before you go out to buy a product. More than half (53 percent) of you want the products you buy to help you express your individuality.[10]

Your preference for choice extends to the work world. Almost half of you (48 percent) say that you won't work for an organization that doesn't offer many different career paths.[11]

life and career expectations

How about your views toward work? There, too, your individual preferences undoubtedly outweigh any common characteristics, but there are a few views that seem to apply to many in your generation. I'll start with your shared ideas about what you *don't* want.

what you don't want: to be part of the traditional workforce

My coauthors and I dedicated our book *Workforce Crisis* to our teenage children. When it was published, my daughter, then sixteen, shared what she thought was a great joke: "You guys," she said conspiratorially, "have just dedicated a book on the *workforce*—to people who never plan to be in one!" Now, despite what it sounds like, I'm (pretty) confident she is not planning a life of leisure. She's an energetic and ambitious young woman, but clearly whatever the word *workforce* triggers in her mind, it does not describe a club she wants to join.

What's going on?

Reactions to the language of work give us some interesting clues about your preferences. Semantics—our interpretation of the meaning of a word—are an important indicator of how values are changing. There seems to be something about words like *workforce* that convey a sense of rigidity and power-based hierarchy that is not appealing to the majority of the Gen Y working-age population.

A key theme of my conversations with Gen Y's is a core frustration with many of the traditional operating policies in large corporations. As highlighted in table 3-1, many of your preferred ways of getting things done are very different from the operating style you find in many large organizations.

You are accustomed to operating in a much more horizontal and networked world than the hierarchical pyramid that is still at the heart of most corporations. You learn, collaborate, and reciprocate within your network, tapping information broadly and offering opinions to anyone you feel will benefit from your insight.

You are used to much more open access to information than you will find inside most corporations. This preference is likely to conflict with the formal policies of the corporation regarding access to information—many designed around corporate concerns for security or privacy—as well as the sense of what older colleagues would consider "proper" business protocol, particularly in formal, hierarchical organizations.

Your views of time and pace differ from the practices you are likely to find. Many of you are amazed by corporations' obsession with time—both the absolute amount spent on work and the

TABLE 3-1

Preferred operating styles: Y's and most corporations

	How Y's would like to operate	How most corporations actually work
Fundamental design	• Collaborative and horizontal more like a loose web than a series of straight lines	• Hierarchical
Source of authority	• Individuals they know and trust (friends, mentors, manager, contacts at previous companies) based on the reputation those individuals have established for reputable knowledge in the specific area.	• Position • Experience-based
Approach to seeking information	• Peer-to-peer first and last • Use Internet for new information • Whatever channel works—let me do it my way	• Authority-based • Hierarchy and tenure-based • Established channels
Information flows and access	• Open • Multiple, reliable sources on the Web and elsewhere, anywhere	• Tightly controlled, often based on concerns about security and privacy
Elapsed time	• Task-based: only enough to get the job done • Focused on completion	• Hour-based; face time for the boss. • Focused on process
Pace and frequency	• Daily interaction; feedback throughout the semester • On their own time	• Reviews once per year
Communication	• Coordination around immediate need on project • Also ongoing, always in touch	• Long-term planning
Path	• Individualized career path based on learning, growth, and challenge	• Up or out
Impact	• Work–life balance more important than almost anything else	• Work defines who you are
Connection and loyalty	• To their friends, mentors, careers	• Assume that the job connects you to the company first

emphasis on specific times: you prefer to work on your own time and at your own pace—flexibly and fast. You are very willing to invest the time required to get the job done, but many of you chafe at the idea of putting in "face time" for the sake of being present or adhering to a fixed, seemingly arbitrary, schedule.

Let's cut to the chase: in many dimensions, most corporations are not compatible with the way you've become accustomed to operating at school and in your interactions with your friends. Most corporate policies were designed by your grandparents' generation. Boomers, by and large, acquiesced to the rules, and, although there have been some important changes over the past decades (for example, the development of horizontal process thinking), many of the fundamental assumptions about how organizations should operate are still based on rules from the mid-1900s: hierarchical structures, rigid, individual-oriented job designs, unilateral employment relationships, and cascading decision making.

The good news for corporations is that many of you seem willing to work within the system to help create change. Worldwide, two-thirds of Y's say they would rather work for one or two companies than for a variety of companies. This is a sharp contrast with X'ers, the quintessential "free-agent nation," whose work philosophy has been characterized by individuality and entrepreneurship. Gen X'ers have proven to be notorious job-hoppers, seeking to round out their own individual experiences. With your generation, chances are good that employers who are willing to meet you halfway will have the opportunity to build a relationship with you.

Despite your preferences, you are not afraid, in general, to move on from a job if it offers no immediate prospect of growth or learning. Our research has found that more than 30 percent of Y's are looking for a new job with a new company at any given time. On average, you predict you will stay in your current job for 4.6 years.[12]

what you want: challenge without traditional responsibility—or your boss's job

You do want significant challenge and meaningful work. Most of you are happy to handle big jobs and tackle them with confidence. Without a doubt, the most engaged Y's in our research were those who felt that they'd been given very challenging assignments. In contrast, in one survey, 75 percent of you said you were unhappy at work; of those, 61 percent said you were bored.[13]

Most of you feel ready to tackle more-complex assignments than you are initially given. Participants in our research were not at all deterred by what older workers might perceive as their lack of experience or even limited qualifications for the task at hand. You think companies underestimate your abilities to scramble to find the necessary guidance for a new task. Most Y's feel sure that they can tap in to appropriate sources to learn how to do what needs to be done. A common complaint from managers is that newly recruited Y's are unwilling to "put in the time" required to learn the ropes. With some tongue in cheek, I advise corporations that the favorite job of any Y is one that is critically important but that he or she has no idea how to do.

At the same time, there's an intriguing trend under way. More people are declining the opportunity to take on more *responsibility*—to move up the corporate ladder. Over a ten-year period, from 1992 to 2002, the desire fell sharply among both men and women of all ages in the workforce for jobs involving greater responsibility. In 2002, only a little more than half of all men and a little more than one-third of all women answered the question, "Would you like a job with more responsibility?" affirmatively.[14]

Broken out by age cohort, only 60 percent of Generation Y said yes in 2002, down from 80 percent of individuals at a similar age ten years earlier. Granted, the oldest among you were only twenty-two at the time and perhaps answering in the context of school. Nonetheless, the attraction of your generation to responsibility seems at first surprisingly low, given your desire for challenging work.

The explanation, I think, comes from your differentiation between "challenge" and "responsibility." As with the word *workforce*, the word *responsibility* connotes a way of working—perhaps conjuring images of bureaucracy, constraints, and answering to other people's rules—that is not appealing to Gen Y.

Consistent with this, many of you are already clear that you don't want your boss's job. We were surprised in our research by the number of Gen Y's who told us their boss's job didn't look "worth it." The trade-off of time and stress versus whatever incremental money or prestige is promised by the next job on the corporate ladder doesn't seem to be a smart deal to many Y's in entry-level corporate jobs.[15]

–A manager schedule is hard—it's a lot to ask, to give up your weekends, screw up your schedule and life, and not get paid enough more to make it worthwhile.

Your challenge rests in finding ways to have the level of impact you desire, doing work that is interesting and meaningful without necessarily getting boxed in to traditional steps on the corporate career path that hold little appeal for you. Companies that want to keep you will have to, among other things, give you ample opportunities to learn and grow experientially through the work you do.

You expect even entry-level jobs to be personally rewarding. This is a particular challenge in industries that have traditionally run on a pyramidal apprentice system, such as law and consulting, in which junior recruits are expected to work long hours on the detailed but often boring background work required by senior partners. One Gen Y attorney notes, "Lots of [law] firms say, 'Oh, we're 150 years old, and we do things like they did 150 years ago. That's not attractive to me. I want to do good work, not just slog through for years till I get my Persian rug and my 50-gallon fish tank."[16]

and what about money . . . and (sigh) debt?

Ah, money.

Attitudes toward money show perhaps the most divergent thinking among Y's around the world. Your economic and cultural experiences—and therefore your expectations about the role money will play in your lives—are quite different.

In a survey of your generation across thirty-three countries, your top three priorities for your next job were interesting work (29 percent), meaningful work (18 percent), and work–life balance (also 18 percent). Financial reward scored fourth, at 14 percent.[17] Worldwide, 56 percent of Y's say that they would give higher priority in choosing work to the ability to pursue their passions, compared with 44 percent who would choose to make lots of money.[18]

But Y's in many parts of the emerging world are eager to participate in the huge leap in consumer wealth that surrounds them. In India, for example, pay is among the most important features of a job. Money connotes value, confers prestige, and provides immediate benefits in the form of a higher standard of living. Indian employees often live with parents and even grandparents and provide as much as 70 percent of the family income. Gen Y's in China also often contribute a significant portion of their family income. However, prestige and connections, reflecting China's relationship-based business world, are considered slightly more important than pay when choosing a job.[19]

Gen Y's growing up in most Western economies have experienced an unprecedented bull market and, for many families, a growing sense of economic prosperity. Coming of age during the most consistently expansive economy in the past thirty years, many of you tend to have a positive, optimistic outlook on life, work, and your economic future. In the United States, the 1990s were a decade of business growth and, at one end of the spectrum, increasing personal wealth, although admittedly a widening socioeconomic gap overall. Although the dot-com bust was also part of the experience of the 1990s, it generally had a more significant impact on X'ers than it did directly on most Y's and their families.

In the United States, your views on money are one of the more hotly debated characteristics of your generation. Although some commentators conclude that money is extremely important to American Y's, in most surveys money ranks lower than other priorities in choosing a career. Most of you say that finding "balance" in life is a higher priority than money alone. A whopping 78 percent of high school students say that "having close family relationships" ranks highest (higher than money and fame, among other things) in defining success.[20]

However, even though many of you say you are not particularly motivated by making *lots* of money, money is nonetheless one of the big challenges you face. Almost one-third (30 percent) of eighteen- to twenty-five-year-olds say debt and finances are the most important problems they face; 73 percent say they have received financial assistance from their parents in the past year.[21]

The debt you carry as a generation is significant. The average debt students incur by the time they leave college (including student loans as well as credit card and other debt) is more than $19,000.[22] Soaring college tuition has forced 65 percent of you to borrow money, compared with only 34 percent who did so thirty years ago when your parents' generation graduated.[23] If you choose to spread your college loan repayments out over thirty years, as many do, you will be between fifty-two and fifty-five on average when you finish paying off your education.

And not too surprisingly, given your debt burden, you are not saving. Fewer than one-third of Y's age eighteen to twenty-five who are eligible for a 401(k) or similar savings plan are actually participating in them; Y's have saved an average of only $3,200 in their 401(k)s.[24]

. . . . .

Have you recognized yourself in these descriptions? At a minimum, they reflect likely assumptions that your workplace colleagues may make about you, based on your generational background.

In part II, I turn to you as an individual and share ways to identify your passions as you search for the work that's likely to be most rewarding to you.

part two

what work is
right for you?

My conversations about writing this book began with Nate.

Home for the holidays, on break from a prestigious university, chock-full of knowledge gained from a great high school experience, he sat down to talk with me about how to shape a book on career strategies for his generation. He began by patiently explaining the obvious.

"First, I'm not likely to read a whole book on that—a blog maybe, but not a book."

"Okay, granted," I said. "But if you were, what would you really like to know about working? What do you wonder about when you think of your career?"

After a thoughtful pause, Nate's answer: "I'd like to know how to get 'enough.'"

Enough. Enough money to lead a reasonable—but not necessarily opulent—lifestyle. Enough time to do the things he enjoys and be with the people he cares about. Enough meaning to feel satisfied that his life work makes a difference.

Not "as much as humanly possible," but "enough."

That's easy to say, but how do you balance all the conflicting priorities? How do you sort through the dizzying possibilities? How do you get to "enough"?

The focus of part II is on you as an individual. You face a series of deeply personal choices—about your preferred lifestyle and location, about money and contribution, about time and structure. Part II is about shaping your personal career strategy. The trick is learning how to make the choices: what criteria to use in separating the good ideas—the ones that are best for *you*—from all the rest.

Most of you will make your choices based on criteria that are very different from those your parents might have used. In the chapters that follow, I talk about six things that you as a Gen Y need to consider—frameworks and questions—as you search for whatever represents "enough" to you in your life. Designed to personalize the ways to plug in—to ensure that you connect where and in the best ways possible for you—these guides incorporate our latest research into why people who enjoy their work do so.

These chapters are designed to help you sort through the options that are both desirable and possible, now and in years ahead, as you continue to make new choices—looking for places where you'll thrive and where you'll comfortably and effectively plug in.

4. find your passion

Do you love what you do—or are planning to do?

If not, you certainly deserve to. As with the quest to find a great life partner—and the pity of settling for a lackluster marriage—you don't need to settle for a work relationship that is only so-so. Not with the shortages of talent that are cropping up all around.

Granted, that question can seem self-indulgent when you're preoccupied with more basic issues: pay the rent and the student loans. Get some health care insurance, if you can. Try to find something to do that you don't hate.

And, to be sure, there are times in your life when those down-to-earth issues will be at the top of your list, particularly as you weather various economic ups and downs. But your generation will be in a favorable position to consider what you really love doing for much of your life; business demand for workers, particularly knowledge workers, will outstrip supply in most of your working years. In addition, backed by strong family support, many of you have the safety net necessary to take some risks, to experiment until you find work that works for you.

In this chapter, I talk about finding work you love—why it's good for you and why it's also important to the success of the organization you join. I help you think about the characteristics of work that you will personally enjoy, and I share the story of one Y who has clearly found his passion.

For those of you who are already in the workplace, take the quiz "Do You Love What You Do?" to see whether you are already doing something you love.

quiz: *do you love what you do?*

1. Are you excited and enthusiastic about your job? [Y] [N]

2. Do you ever lose yourself—forget about time and place—because you're so wrapped up in the work you truly enjoy? [Y] [N]

3. Do you happily focus on your work, versus waiting eagerly for the next e-mail or IM to arrive and break the boredom? [Y] [N]

4. Do you voluntarily invest extra effort or produce significantly more than your work requires? [Y] [N]

5. Is what you're doing so inherently interesting that you think about it after hours—for example, in the car or on the way home? [Y] [N]

6. Do you routinely search for ways to improve things at work or volunteer for more difficult assignments? [Y] [N]

7. Is your enthusiasm contagious—does your passion for work encourage others to join in? [Y] [N]

8. Are you proud to identify with your work? [Y] [N]

If you answered no to more than three of these questions, you're not enjoying your work nearly enough. You can do better—maybe not immediately, but soon.

I'd like you to meet one Y who loves what he does.

siamak's story: a passionate gen y

Siamak Taghaddos is a Y who, at age twenty-six, is passionate about his work.[1] With a partner, Siamak founded GotVMail Communications, which offers an award-winning virtual phone system designed for entrepreneurs and small business owners. The company helps its clients sound professional by creating a virtual office that connects callers to employees wherever they are, on any type of phone—home, office, VoIP, or mobile—without the need to purchase or maintain any equipment. In 2006 GotVMail was sixty-sixth on *Inc.* magazine's list of the top five hundred fastest-growing companies in the United States.

Born 1981 in Tehran, Iran, Siamak moved with his family to the United States as a teenager. His diverse, bicultural background sharpened his ability to empathize with the specific needs of many different people and exposed him to a broad array of ideas—a rich set of options from which to choose ones that will work best for the needs of his business.

Siamak's father was an entrepreneur, always experimenting. Siamak remembers some of the best moments of his childhood as ones in which he was engaged in hands-on activities with his father—building a table, fixing computers, and other tasks that gave him the confidence to pick issues apart and put them back together. That feeling of building, changing the component pieces, and creating something new is one that Siamak re-creates as he finds his passion in work.

His own entrepreneurial interests have been evident since high school, where he started a Web-based business selling pagers at a discount to kids who couldn't otherwise afford them. For college, he chose Babson, well known for its outstanding entrepreneurship programs. By eighteen he was well on his way to understanding the characteristics of the work that would reflect his passions.

Siamak strongly believes that you'll be successful only if you do something you love, and something that "serves who *you* are." He wants to do something significant—and different. His philosophy is to stand out but preserve tradition along the way. Believing that any business is closely tied to the reputation of its founder, Siamak cares deeply about creating a firm that is highly professional, well respected, and proudly associated with his family. Siamak believes that too many people start companies for the sole purpose of making money.

Siamak's early experience with pulling things apart and re-thinking how they work is reflected in his business. His philosophy in all aspects of the business is to ask, "If I want to do something best, how could I also do it differently?" This applies not only to services that directly touch the firm's customers, but also to all aspects of how he and his partner, David Hauser, run the company. For example, they devised a virtual lunch program by finding a local company with an online interface and providing a company subsidy to allow GotVMail's employees a discount. His practical goal was to find a way for his employees to have lunch without a huge expense (to them or to the company) and without wasting large stretches of time to go out. In addition to meeting these goals, he was able to do it in a distinctive way that reinforces the fundamental values of the firm: technology driven, service oriented, high quality, and efficient.

Siamak is hands-on, believing you can shape a great company only by doing everything yourself the first time. Nothing goes on at GotVMail that one of the two business partners has not done first. They learn what works, make mistakes, understand the limitations of the process, develop the approach that fits their business model, and *then* pass the activity to others. Siamak hires employees based on their fit with the firm's values.

Like many of you, Siamak favors action over planning: "I don't plan. If I need to do something, I just get it done. If I see any employee walking by, I just talk to him or her and get it done. I'm always on my feet—always changing things. I make a decision quickly and then help people understand why."

Siamak feels the biggest question for Generation Y is what he terms the "Google algorithm." How will you filter through all the possibilities you face? How do you pick the right things? If you go only to the same stores that everyone else goes to, it's hard to develop a unique style. He advises that picking and choosing should be about exploring and finding the unique thing that is right for you. To get there, try things yourself—put the time and effort into things you like—and the end result will be something you'll do with pride.

And, perhaps more important, live for today. Siamak views himself as a lucky person: "With world events, at any point in time, my life could be over—so never live in the future and never live in the past. Live for today."

Passionately.

plug in: get engaged with work you love

Many members of your grandparents' generation worked on assembly lines in a manufacturing economy for forty years or more before retiring for a well-deserved rest—or at least a break from the monotony of that work. They paid their dues, collected a steady salary, and racked up retirement benefits. I doubt that "enjoyment" was a big part of the equation, except maybe the satisfaction that came from providing for their families.

You face a different set of prospects. Our economy is increasingly dominated by either professional craft- or knowledge-based jobs; it's not that they can't be dreary, as well, but the possibility of finding work that you truly enjoy has never been greater. Don't settle for less. Loving your work, pursuing your passion—or being "engaged" in your work, as is commonly said in business today—is a special way to live.

Interestingly, this hasn't always been the prevailing view. For many people in the past, work was work and fun was fun, and never the two did meet. Older generations typically did not approach finding work the way I'm encouraging you to—to begin by seeking your passion.

Given that, it's perhaps not surprising that most people are *not* highly engaged in their work. Today, on average, only about 20 percent of the global workforce is highly engaged. Almost 20 percent are at the other end of the spectrum—actively bitter. And about 60 percent are somewhere in the middle—going through the motions. These same proportions are roughly true within the U.S. workforce. Among you Gen Y's who are already working, 42 percent of you think your jobs are "just okay" and a surprising 33 percent of you say you "can't stand" your jobs.[2]

Engagement is not the same as satisfaction. Satisfaction with work focuses on what makes you "not unhappy"—adequate benefits, a safe and nondiscriminatory work environment, reasonable pay, and so on. Engagement is about being deeply committed to and energized by your work. As one executive put it, "Engagement is an active, proactive, discretionary effort; satisfaction is entitlement, moving along year to year, looking for retirement." Another defined the difference between engagement and satisfaction as "the difference between giving and getting."[3]

And, lest anyone say that it's a bit self-centered to think about finding work you love, actually, nothing could be further from the truth. You owe it to yourself *and* to your employer to choose work that you feel passionately about. Corporate leaders are coming to understand that "buying bodies and hands" just isn't enough. Hearts and minds are essential. Business success requires creativity, teamwork, and commitment. These intangibles come when you *choose* to contribute them. When you are engaged.

When engagement is lacking, companies suffer financially, often plagued by high turnover, poor treatment of customers, and a lack of innovative ideas.[4] Organizations that foster and sustain engagement realize major returns on those efforts: improved shareholder value; higher levels of productivity and profitability; and increased organizational stability. This level of success undoubtedly comes from the high levels of "discretionary effort": passionate employees *choose* to invest more energy and initiative than would be needed only to get by.

It's a win/win—for you and for the organization you join—to take the time to find work you love.

Before I ask you to think about your own passions, let's make sure we're on the same page—imagining the same feeling. Here are two analogies for engagement that you have probably already experienced in other parts of your life.

flow

Have you ever been so deeply "into" something—an athletic activity perhaps, or playing music—that the moment stands out as one of the best in your life? That the activity feels almost effortless?

Try to remember a time in your life when you've felt

✓ Completely involved, focused, and concentrating

✓ A sense of ecstasy, of being outside everyday reality

✓ Great inner clarity, knowing what needs to be done and how well it is going

✓ Confidence that your skills are adequate to the task, and feeling neither anxious nor bored

✓ Serene, with no worries

✓ Thoroughly focused on the present, without the awareness of time passing

✓ Intrinsically motivated, meaning that doing the activity was its own reward

This type of rich experience has been called "flow."[5]

Much of the work that has been done to understand the experience of flow and to help people achieve it has been done in sports. Many top athletes recognize the critical importance of being in this state—what they often refer to as being "in the zone"—in order to perform at peak levels.

There are several important lessons to take away from the work that has been done with flow that you can use as you think about finding flow at work.

First, flow is not the same as pure pleasure. Pleasure does not involve a sense of achievement or active contribution to the result, but flow does. Therefore, don't look only for something you enjoy; it needs to be something that also gives you a sense of pride and accomplishment.

Second, one of the key insights is that flow occurs only when the challenge you face is in balance with your skills. Work that is far too difficult can cause anxiety; work that is far too easy leads quickly to boredom. Flow is a paradoxical kind of condition in which you're operating on a fine line; you can just (barely) do what needs to be done. Look for work that stretches your abilities but does not make you feel overwhelmed.

Sadly, as with engagement surveys, assessments of flow show that only about 20 percent of people around the world experience this feeling on a regular basis.

energy

Tapping in to multiple sources of energy is another analogy for being fully engaged. Great athletes, of course, achieve maximum performance by harnessing not only physical energy but also mental, emotional, and—for many—spiritual energy. The same is true for people who excel at their work. Consider looking for work that will tap all your energy resources.

Thinking of engagement in this way is a reminder of three important elements that need to be part of any successful work experience—all of which relate to how you will build and manage your energy capacity as part of your work routines. Plugging in at peak engagement is not something that happens naturally, without practice, and it's not something you can do endlessly, with no opportunities to recharge.

This energy analogy reminds us that full engagement:

✓ Requires that energy "investments" be balanced with energy "deposits." As you tap in to your individual energy, your supply is inevitably drawn down. You'll need to rebuild your energy supplies when they are low. This means that your periods of full engagement need to be offset by periods of strategic disengagement to restore the energy you've expended.

✓ Requires that people push beyond normal limits, "training" like an elite athlete every day. Look for work that will allow you to challenge yourself a bit more each day. However, just as in physical exercise, the more you exceed your normal limits, the longer your recovery time will be.

✓ Benefits from positive rituals—precise behaviors that become automatic over time. Think about the way elite athletes often rely on rituals, from the way they manage their emotions under stress to the sort of mental preparation routines they develop. For example, golfers often go through exactly the same steps before each putt. At work, rituals should focus on *doing* rather than not doing; an example of a positive ritual is, "I will check my e-mail at three specific times a day" rather than, "I will stop checking my e-mail so often."

Your ability to engage may be enhanced through training but is never endless. A key question you have to answer is, Based on your deepest values, beliefs, and preference, what work *deserves* to get your full engagement?

your personal life lures

The summer before I went to college, I had a great job working for a weekly newspaper in a little midwestern town. Life at a small-town weekly was never dull and never the same two days in a row. It also had a distinct pattern: adrenaline-soaked near-crisis-level activity, followed by days of near leisure. The crescendo would build over the week—as I first chatted with the local merchants and sold ad space, covered town events, wrote the stories, designed the ads—and then peaked on the day before publication, with an all-night flurry of last-minute activity and a wild race to the printer. Whew. Then we would get a very late start the next morning, with coffee and doughnuts all around.

Years later, when I began to think about getting my first "real" job, I knew that what I really wanted was a job that mimicked that crazy newsroom—intense pressure, followed by downtime and reflection—as well as the ability to juggle multiple tasks at once. I wanted the sense of entrepreneurship and individual achievement; I loved the blend of selling, writing, and design-ing that was rolled into that one job. I found just that in a ca-reer in management consulting. As with Siamak, the work I loved had its seeds in activities I had loved when I was younger, even though the eventual manifestation of those activities was quite different.

Not all of us find the same work environment attractive. What we enjoy—what causes us to feel comfortable and puts us in a frame of mind to do our best work—varies from person to person.

The key to finding work you love is figuring out what you personally value most highly—what I call your *life lures:* the work experience that will create flow and tap your energy. Understanding your life lures should usefully serve as the basis for your work choices.

To begin, think about specific situations in your past in which you have felt the ways described in each line of the exercise in table 4-2.

Describe each situation in as much detail as possible. Were you:

✓ Working with a team, with one other person, or on your own?

✓ Doing something that you were winning at, that was directly benefiting others, that was fun?

✓ Engaging in something that you knew how to do well and for which the outcome was reasonably predictable, or inventing as you went along, doing something that involved some high-stakes risk?

What other descriptors of the experience stand out in your mind? Make notes in this exercise; use it to collect your ideas.

. . . . .

Finding what is engaging for you is a highly personal quest. What causes people to feel engaged differs significantly from

TABLE 4-2

Remember a time . . . : The characteristics of times when you were engaged

Remember a time . . .	What exactly was I doing?	What were the characteristics of the situation?
When you were excited and enthusiastic about something you were doing		
When you "lost yourself"—forgetting about time and place—as you did something		
When you resisted distractions for a significant period of time		
When you invested discretionary effort to produce significantly more than the task required, working all kinds of hours to get things done and done right		
When you found the challenge so inherently interesting that you pondered it happily even when not directly engaged in it—perhaps in the car on the way home or in the morning shower		

(continued)

TABLE 4-2 (*continued*)

Remember a time . . . : The characteristics of times when you were engaged

Remember a time . . .	What exactly was I doing?	What were the characteristics of the situation?
When you developed creative new ways to do the work or searched for ways to improve things rather than just react to an obvious approach		
When you volunteered for the more difficult assignment		
When you were contagious, meaning you shared your enthusiasm with others in ways that encouraged them to join in—when you recruited others to the activity		
When you proudly identified with the activity and told others that this was what you did		

individual to individual. We are excited and intrigued by different values. Some of you care deeply about social connections and friendships you can form. Others care about the opportunity for creative expression. Still others want to make as much money as possible in as flexible, low-commitment a way as possible. Some of you want to give back to others or make a lasting difference in the world.

We also like to work in very different ways. Some people prefer open-ended tasks, others, highly structured tasks. Some like to work on teams, and others, independently. Some need and enjoy a great deal of day-to-day guidance. Others work best when left alone to solve an ambiguous challenge.

We are excited and attracted by different career paths and goals. Some people have high tolerance for risk, and love the rush of a high-risk, high-reward environment. Others crave the steady dependability of a well-structured, long-term climb up the career ladder.

In the next chapter, I talk about how to translate the characteristics of situations you love, those you've just identified in the chart, into your life lures.

5. identify your preferences

What does the process of pursuing your passion look like? What's the next step down that path?

The good news is that it's not nearly as nebulous as you might think. Our research has shown that there is a clear link between understanding what you love and identifying tangible elements of the work environment that would be best for you.

out of the starting gate

Imagine that you're in the job market, with offers in hand from three firms. All three are attractive—the type of opportunities you've been looking for, with competitive compensation packages. You decide to meet with each firm one more time, specifically to talk about what your entry experience might be like—what to expect in your first six months on the job. Here's what representatives from the three companies say. Which job will you take?

Company A: Probation and a Team Voting Approach

Actually, your first month will be a probationary period in which you'll get to know and work closely with your assigned teammates. They'll see how well you work with the group and contribute to its success. At the end of that period, your teammates—your peers—will vote on whether or not you will get to stay in the organization.

Company B: Fishbowl Challenge Approach

We can't tell you what your exact role will be or who you'll be working with. For the first three months, you'll be in our "fishbowl," performing a series of weekly challenges, perhaps designing new products or marketing campaigns, under the close scrutiny of our CEO and other senior executives. At the end of the time, depending on what we observe, we'll help you find the right position for your skills.

Company C: Training and Apprentice Approach

Your first three months will be spent learning our way of doing business. We have a specific way of operating, and we expect you to follow our processes closely. We're convinced that the ways we've outlined are the most productive and successful. After an extensive training program, you'll get a chance to apprentice with one of our strongest performers.

If you're like most people, these three ways of starting work at a new company are not equally appealing. In fact, I suspect most of you would probably have a distinct preference for one over the others.

If social relationships at work are important to you, if team-work is something you enjoy and believe you excel at, then the first offer would probably sound good. The entry process certainly drives home the point that this is a company that puts a high priority on team behavior.

If you love the challenge of creating new things and see work as a platform to express yourself, and if you have a high tolerance for ambiguity, then the second company might be for you. Again, the entry process sets a clear tone—intense challenge, high visibility, and a chance to show what you can do.

If clearly specified tasks are important to you, and if you want a well-defined path to succeed at work, then the third company probably sounds like a dream come true. Clearly the management has thought about how to do well and is prepared to invest significant time and resources in helping you learn the ropes.

Getting it right—finding a work environment that matches your personality and preferences—is key to your ultimate enjoyment of your work. In the end, the role you will be asked to play and the characteristics of the workplace need to be in line with the role you're *prepared* to play and the environment you enjoy. By choosing the company that is best suited to your needs and preferences, you increase the chances you will find yourself in a place that matches your passions, one in which you will be highly engaged in your work.

moving down the path toward your ideal job

Let's take the second step in finding work you will love and that will work for you. Keeping in mind the situations you identified in chapter 4, those in which you felt highly engaged or passionate, the next step is to identify the practical characteristics of your ideal relationship with work and the pragmatic clues that will help you find it. Our research has shown that there is a high correlation between certain types of passion—certain life lures—and specific, identifiable elements of the work environment. For example, someone with a passion for creating unique items with lasting value—let's say by designing buildings or writing books—is much more likely to prefer flexible schedules and independence than someone whose passion is leading teams successfully into competition.

My colleagues' and my research has identified six *archetypes* of work-related passions and preferred relationships with work.[1] They describe the six roles that work plays in our lives and represent six life lures.

- ✓ **Expressive legacy:** Work is about creating something of lasting value.

- ✓ **Secure progress:** Work is about predictable upward mobility—a secure path to success.

- ✓ **Individual expertise and team victory:** Work is an opportunity to contribute, to be a valuable part of a winning team.

✓ **Risk with reward:** Work is an opportunity for challenge, change, learning, and, maybe, wealth.

✓ **Flexible support:** Work is a livelihood but not currently a priority.

✓ **Limited obligations:** Work's value is largely its near-term economic gain.

Take the ten-question assessment in table 5-1. Which of the statements in each row of the assessment do you identify with most closely? Once you've completed the assessment, turn to table 5-2 at the end of the chapter to see which lure is most important to you.

Once you have your results, the following descriptions of each lure will help you identify the observable criteria you should use as you evaluate your work options.

Note that some of the criteria apply to the nature of the tasks you would perform, and others apply to the work environment—the type of organization you would be a part of, the management style of the boss, and so on. You'll find that organizations differ widely in important components of the work experience, often even within an industry. For example, some companies have risk-based compensation (options, bonuses), whereas others have predictable cost-of-living-based salary structures. Some organizations set up highly flexible, self-scheduling work groups; others take an intense "all hands on deck" approach most of the time. Some reflect an underlying philosophy of paternalism; others operate with a virtually contractor-like, hands-off attitude. Your criteria should encompass the nature of both the work and the workplace.

TABLE 5-1

What engages you?

Which of the following statements do you identify with most closely? In each row, select the box or boxes that most closely match your preferences or feelings about work. Once you've completed the assessment, total the number of times you've selected the statements in each column. Match the column(s) with the highest score to the lures in table 5-2.

	A	B	C	D	E	F
I like performing tasks when . . .	. . . the task itself is ambiguous and I personally need to figure out both what it might become and how to do it.	. . . the approach for doing the task well has been determined by others and taught to me.	. . . my team collectively possesses the skills and knowledge to perform the task, although I may know only one piece.	. . . how to do the task is unknown and open ended, requiring that we pioneer new approaches.	. . . how to do the task well is clear and easy to learn.	. . . the task is easy.
I prefer work arrangements that . . .	. . . allow me complete individual latitude.	. . . are well defined and traditional (9 to 5).	. . . include regular hours that align the schedules of all team members and promote face time.	. . . are highly flexible in both time and place and provide time to pursue external adventures.	. . . allow me to shift my schedule on a daily basis, as needed to balance my other responsibilities.	. . . are short term.
I like work that . . .	. . . is extremely stimulating, requiring creativity and providing opportunity to learn and grow.	. . . is challenging, but within my current capabilities based on the training I've received.	. . . builds on my area of expertise and allows me to contribute my competence for collective good.	. . . is extremely challenging and varied and never involves doing the same thing twice.	. . . is straight-forward and has well-defined routines that I can plug in and out of, with others picking up where needed.	. . . doesn't involve a lot of dumb questions from customers or colleagues.

	A	B	C	D	E	F
I get really psyched by . . .	. . . opportunities to build or create something with lasting value.	. . . being on a steady road to success, with training and development along the way.	. . . having fun with my colleagues—working hard together and celebrating.	. . . interacting with really bright people and recognized thought leaders.	. . . dreaming of how I'll plunge into work later in life, when my current external responsibilities are lessened.	. . . a paycheck with some overtime or a bonus payment.
In my life, work. . . .	. . . is my opportunity to have a lasting impact on someone or something.	. . . is my route to upward mobility and economic security.	. . . is a major source of pride, based on our winning track record and my contributions to the team's success.	. . . is an adrenaline rush, one of multiple opportunities for adventure and thrills.	. . . is less important to me at the moment than my other responsibilities and interests.	. . . honestly, a hassle.
It is important to me to have a manager who . . .	. . . helps me line up the resources I need for my work, leaves me alone to do it, keeps the bureaucrats away, and "promotes" my work when it's complete.	. . . is clear and up front with expectations, ties my compensation to fair goals, respects my tenure, and follows through on promises.	. . . knows how to create a strong team, resolves any interpersonal conflicts quickly and competently, and acts as a player/coach to get the job done successfully.	. . . lets me do new things based on my interests, treats me like an individual, gets rid of incompetent colleagues, and knows how to have fun.	. . . understands that life is complicated for me now, is empathic and willing to help me arrange a flexible schedule, but sees my longer-term potential.	. . . is competent, fair, and pays me for the work I do.

(continued)

TABLE 5-1 (continued)

What engages you?

Which of the following statements do you identify with most closely? Select the box or boxes that most closely match your preferences or feelings about work.

	A	B	C	D	E	F
It is important to me to work for an organization that . . .	. . . does work that creates things of lasting value or that have social significance.	. . . is financially stable and secure.	. . . is known for its excellence and wins in the marketplace.	. . . is "hot" and carries the possibility of significant financial upside.	. . . values its employees and has a caring employee value proposition.	. . . pays well and isn't full of jerks.
One of the things I would consider about a possible new employer is . . .	. . . whether it would provide me with a platform for self-realization and the freedom to be entrepreneurial.	. . . the quality of the long-term career development options—whether they represent a steady, predictable path to success.	. . . the extent to which my area of competence would contribute to the organization's success.	. . . the opportunity for personal financial upside through bonus and stock.	. . . the degree to which it would be possible to establish highly flexible arrangements, including, preferably, self-scheduling.	. . . whether the hiring process is quick and easy, with few required qualifications.
A deal breaker for me in selecting a job would be if . . .	. . . I wouldn't be empowered to do the best work possible in the way I think it needs to be done.	. . . the compensation philosophy didn't seem fair, including retirement benefits you can count on.	. . . the environment did not promote collaboration and teamwork.	. . . the deal did not offer the possibility of significant upside compensation.	. . . the deal did not include generous vacation policies and cafeteria-style benefits so I could get the type of support I most need.	. . . it did not offer me a higher wage than the company down the street.

	A	B	C	D	E	F
I feel I am successful in my work if . . .	. . . I am being true to myself, expressing myself by doing something I feel is of value.	. . . I am making steady progress up the career ladder and saving for retirement.	. . . my team wins and I have made a contribution to our shared success.	. . . I am always learning and growing through exciting new assignments.	. . . my activities outside work don't suffer, because they are currently far more important than this job.	. . . the boss singles me out for a spot bonus because of something I did today.
Total number of responses selected in column	___	___	___	___	___	___

expressive legacy

Individuals who identify closely with this archetype tend to have the following characteristics:

- ✓ They care about building something of lasting value.

- ✓ They are entrepreneurial, hardworking, creative, well educated, and self-motivated.

- ✓ They consider themselves leaders and love to assume responsibility.

- ✓ They are the most likely to define success as being true to themselves.

- ✓ They say they will never retire.

- ✓ They place less value on traditional rewards—such as compensation, vacation time, or even a better benefits package—than many others do.

- ✓ They are looking for work that continues to empower and stimulate them, enables them to continue to learn and grow, and has a greater social purpose.

If you share the values of this archetype, use the following criteria to judge your future work possibilities. Consider each of your options in terms of the degree to which it offers the following:

- ✓ Individual latitude; the ability to be your own boss

- ✓ The requirement to be creative in order to succeed

✓ Ongoing opportunities to learn and grow, ideally through continual exposure to bright colleagues, stimulating ideas, and leading-edge issues

✓ The opportunity for your work to have a lasting impact on someone or something

Examples of the type of work that is often engaging for individuals in this archetype include architecture (creating something of lasting value), construction (individual latitude), professional services (stimulating work), and a wide variety of the arts. Attractive work environments include self-employment and entrepreneurial start-ups.

Companies that want to attract and retain people who place a high priority on the nature of the work itself—on creating something of lasting value—often do things that strongly reflect the company's heritage, values, and ambitions in unique and memorable ways. Bright Horizons, a provider of employer-sponsored child care, uses a high-touch recruiting process that emphasizes the lasting impact an early childhood educator can have on young lives. A walk through Xilinx's hall of patents or past the mural depicting the founders' early vision for programmable logic devices leaves any visitor with a sense of the firm's grand ambition. Look for these kinds of signals if expressive legacy describes you.

secure progress

Individuals in this archetype have the following characteristics:

✓ They seek upward mobility—a steady, predictable path to success.

✓ They pride themselves on being highly reliable and loyal workers.

✓ They value fair, traditional rewards, including concrete compensation, good benefits, and a solid, predictable retirement package.

✓ They are uncomfortable with risky or highly variable compensation, including stock and bonuses.

✓ They like to work hard.

✓ They place high value on their family.

✓ They have less interest in "softer" work benefits such as stimulating work, enjoyable workplaces, work that is worthwhile to society, or flexible work arrangements.

✓ They seek stable and secure environments and tend to have long tenures with one employer.

If you share the values of this archetype, look for opportunities that offer the following:

✓ Fair, predictable rewards

✓ Concrete compensation, benefits, and a solid retirement package

✓ Stable, secure work environments; for example, investigate the company's financial history and business outlook

✓ Work that features structure and routine

✓ Career-related training

Examples of careers that are often engaging for individuals in this archetype include those in education, health care, government, manufacturing, and transportation. Look in particular for firms that can offer a predictable, upward path to success and economic security (and note that many simply can't make this promise). Be alert to evidence that the company is committed to employees' long-term security; for example, ExxonMobil made the decision to stick with defined benefit pension plans several years ago, recognizing the importance of security in the firm's employee experience. The Container Store's investment in training—more than five times the industry average—and clearly articulated progressions emphasize its strong commitment to structured career development.

individual expertise and team victory

Individuals in this archetype have the following characteristics:

- ✓ They enjoy being part of a winning team and seek an atmosphere that is cooperative.

- ✓ They care deeply about being highly competent at the work they do and contributing to the organization's success.

- ✓ They take pride in their work and are willing to put in extra effort.

- ✓ They are loyal, hardworking, reliable, capable, and typically very experienced.

- ✓ They place less value than most others do on individual rewards such as more money or vacation, and they express less need for flexible work arrangements.

✓ They place strong emphasis on work that is personally stimulating, work environments that are congenial and fun, colleagues who cooperate, and employers who provide stability and job security.

If you share the values of this archetype, look for opportunities that offer the following:

✓ Work that involves teaming with others

✓ Workplaces that value fun

✓ Work approaches that are designed for collaboration

✓ Stable, well-organized, and well-run environments

✓ Competent colleagues

✓ Work that leverages and builds your existing personal strengths

The particular industry is less important to individuals in this archetype than is finding a team-based work environment. Many seek managerial roles.

If you want to work in a team-based environment, look for specific practices within the firm that require or support team-based behavior. The Royal Bank of Scotland is well known for its every-morning management meetings, in which goals for the day are set collaboratively by the top executives. Whole Foods' hiring and compensation processes are team-based; candidates are on probation until the team votes that they may be hired full-time.

risk with reward

Individuals in this archetype have the following characteristics:

✓ They seek lives filled with change and adventure, and they see work as one of multiple opportunities to experience a thrill.

✓ They tend to be well educated and have a strong preference for working with other bright people.

✓ They thrive on exciting work.

✓ They enjoy assuming positions of responsibility.

✓ They are driven by variety and opportunities for growth.

✓ They want to do work that is inherently worthwhile.

✓ They pioneer new ways of working.

✓ They are the most likely to want flexible workplaces and schedules that enable them to work on their own terms and pursue their own interests.

✓ They are confident in their abilities and are the most likely to seek out bonus compensation and stock as rewards for their accomplishments.

✓ They own their careers and actively explore their career options; their tenures with employers on average are brief.

If you share the values of this archetype, look for opportunities that offer the following:

✓ Opportunities for personal financial upside—bonuses and stock

✓ Flexible workplaces and schedules based on your own terms

✓ Opportunities to choose assignments from a wide menu of options

✓ Opportunities to change tasks frequently

✓ Open-ended tasks and approaches

✓ Frequent exposure to other bright people and recognized thought leaders

Examples of work environments that can be engaging for individuals who fit the risk with reward archetype include those in information technology, investment banking, and professional services. Many of these individuals are frequently happiest working for smaller organizations or being self-employed.

Look for firms that clearly signal a commitment to challenge, change, learning, and the possibility of wealth, at every turn. Trilogy, a software firm, uses a highly challenging orientation process to create this culture from the start.

flexible support

Individuals in this archetype have the following characteristics:

✓ They see work as a source of livelihood but not currently a primary focus in their lives.

✓ They are typically pursuing interests and priorities outside work and are trying to create balance in their lives— personally, financially, and emotionally.

✓ They are looking for employers that can make it a little easier to cope—for example, by offering a flexible menu of benefit options that fit their specific needs.

✓ They value environments that are congenial and fun.

✓ They tend to view their nonwork activities as temporary and think they may want to devote more time and energy to their work in the future, but for now are seeking roles at work that will enable them to have control of both their careers and their lives.

If you share the values of this archetype, look for opportunities that offer the following:

✓ Highly flexible work arrangements, including, to the extent possible, options for self-scheduling

✓ Generous vacation or options for leave

✓ Flexible benefit programs, preferably in a cafeteria-style offering that allows choice among child care, elder care, and other options based on your specific needs

✓ Work with well-defined routines—the ability to "plug in" and out again with ease

✓ Work that can be done virtually and does not require direct personal interaction

✓ Work environments that are congenial, empathic, and fun

Examples of work environments that are often engaging for individuals in this archetype include backroom work in financial services and leisure and hospitality, because both often offer the scheduling options this group desires. Look for human resource practices that emphasize an organization's flexibility and empathy. JetBlue's system for its reservation agents allows them to work at home and self-schedule within their work group, an example of competing for talent on the basis of maximum flexibility.

limited obligations

Individuals who fit the limited obligations profile have the following characteristics (and given these characteristics, chances are they're probably not reading this book!):

✓ They see the value of work largely in terms of near-term economic gain.

✓ They prefer work that makes minimal demands on their time.

✓ They place high value on traditional compensation and benefits packages.

✓ They express less interest than other segments in work that is enjoyable, personally stimulating, or worthwhile to society.

If you share the values of this archetype, look for opportunities that offer the following:

✓ Low barriers to entry—hiring processes that are quick and easy, and jobs that are relatively easy to come by and learn

✓ Work that has well-defined routines

✓ Traditional compensation and lucrative benefits packages

✓ Stability and security

✓ Opportunities for periodic recognition

Examples of work environments that might be best suited to individuals in this archetype, largely because the positions have low barriers to entry, include retail, wholesale, and transportation.

. . . . .

The criteria associated with your life lure should be part of your reflections as you evaluate work opportunities. They will help you increase the odds of finding a career where you can really plug in.

In summary, these criteria ask you to consider four different aspects of each opportunity—what I call the "four C's":

✓ **Content:** The nature of the task itself—whether it's well defined or ambiguous, done at a pace that is fast or leisurely, requires a high degree of team interaction or can be done individually, and so on

✓ **Compensation:** What you want, broadly, in return—the mix of salary, benefits, deferred compensation, learning opportunities, satisfaction from giving back, pleasure from social networks, or other benefits that you value most from work

✓ **Connection:** How you want to interact with the company—for example, whether as an employee or in a freelance relationship, with a lot or a little management oversight, with frequent feedback or more formal reviews, or in a management style that is hierarchical or participative

✓ **Communication:** The core values you care about and want to share with the organization and its leaders

As you think about what you want to do next, it's important to think about these preferences. If you don't get this right, no matter how much you intellectually like the idea of the work, you almost certainly won't be engaged. If you took the self-assessment in table 5-1, check out table 5-2, which identifies your life lures based on the answers you gave.

In the next chapter, I talk about some of the places where you might be most likely to find your ideal work and work environment—and how those places are changing.

TABLE 5-2

Your life lures

Column A	*Expressive legacy:* Work is about creating something of lasting value.
Column B	*Secure progress:* Work is about upward mobility, a predictable, upward path to success.
Column C	*Individual expertise and team victory:* Work is an opportunity to be a contributing member of a winning team.
Column D	*Risk with reward:* Work is an opportunity for challenge, change, learning, and, maybe, wealth.
Column E	*Flexible support:* Work generates a livelihood but not currently a life priority.
Column F	*Limited obligations:* Work's value is largely its near-term economic gain.

6. target your place

Where are you likely to find a career that taps your passions and matches your preferences? What place offers the life lures you've identified and an environment that meets your preferences for how you'd like to work?

Many of you say you're not planning a career within corporations—at least not in other people's corporations! Yours is a generation of entrepreneurs and independent adventurers, of activists and artists. You want to make a difference, have an impact, and do meaningful work now. Where is that most likely to be possible?

Although there's no absolute answer, certain outcomes are more probable in some places than in others. Some places are more likely to provide long-term stability than others. Some are more likely to allow you greater degrees of flexibility. Some offer higher average incomes than others, although they are likely to require significant investments of time. Some have great inherent uncertainty or require more creativity or even raw talent.

And almost all of them are changing. The arenas I focus on are ones in which some of the stereotypical characteristics are changing the most.

✓ *Corporations* are evolving into next-generation enterprises.

✓ *Entrepreneurial start-ups* are facing better odds.

✓ *Professional services* are rethinking the one-size-fits-all career model.

✓ *Education* is challenging itself to match twenty-first-century needs.

✓ *Social entrepreneurship and nonprofits* are doing good and doing well.

✓ *The trades and other so-called middle-skill jobs* are not going away.

✓ *Government services* are offering unprecedented opportunity.

There are other possibilities that I won't cover in detail. Many of you are attracted to the arts—film, music, culinary arts, the-ater, or other creative expressions. The issues here are pretty self-evident. Do you have the talent? And are you willing and realistically able, in terms of time and money, to endure the dif-ficulties of building your portfolio and reputation, particularly since these arenas are likely to be highly competitive, given the number of your contemporaries headed in similar directions?

A career in the military offers a number of well-known advantages in access to education and financial security. The agriculture sector is small in terms of available jobs but offers independence akin to entrepreneurship.

This chapter is about thinking broadly—considering a wide range of possible places in which to begin or further your career, including those opportunities that exist outside the conventional "get your first job in a big company" route.

As you do, don't fall prey to stereotypes. Corporations are becoming less rigid; start-ups are not (quite) as risky as they used to be. Professional service firms are offering multiple career paths. A century-old approach to education is facing change. The trades are neither low paying nor disappearing. Government service does not always equate with bureaucracy.

corporations large and small: evolving into next-generation enterprises

Corporations have lots of advantages as places to begin your career. Many of them offer great learning opportunities, significant variety, and attractive rewards. But, to be honest, there is still a pretty high likelihood of a mismatch between what many of you want and the specifics that some corporations are offering. The challenge you face in finding a corporate job is evaluating the *specific* opportunity you'll be given and the work environment you'll be part of (in chapter 8, I talk more about how to do this).

Many Y's are uncomfortable with the old corporate rules. One of you responded to one of my blog posts this way.

Corporate life needs a major makeover to become more attractive to both X'ers and the generation below them. Current corporate life is still very much a product of mechanistic Taylorian thinking that dates back to the early 20th century and saw employees as automata . . . [F]or people who want to retain their individuality, who want to bring their personality, their interests, their emotional needs into the workplace, the big corporation is not likely to be a particularly appealing place. . . . To appeal to the under 40's, the corporation has got to move on from Frederick Taylor and notions of control, and take a few lessons from the world of the social networks.

Happily, most corporations *are* changing and will continue to change in substantial ways over the upcoming years—and you can help them do so. Although it will take a bit of finesse to plug in to some of these environments, these are organizations that really need you.

Corporations, by and large, are built on a premise that there will be a few people at the top (even more basically, that there *is* a "top") making key decisions and setting strategy, a medium number of people in the middle translating strategy into day-to-day operations, and a lot of workers at the bottom of the pyramid who are more or less doing as instructed.

But things are happening. Technology is facilitating organizations that are more networked and horizontal. The economy is shifting toward knowledge work, the way companies make money is evolving, and, with this, the way work gets done is changing, too. As one of you said, the Web sites you use in your personal life "have one thing in common: users control them . . . Gen Y is bringing decentralized organizations mainstream."[1]

I agree. You can influence the direction of change if you're smart.

the shape of enterprises to come

By 2025, most corporations will operate as what my colleagues and I have termed *next-generation enterprises*: connected communities encompassing a wide variety of partners and contractor relationships (see figure 6-1). These corporate communities will be intensely collaborative, continually informed, technologically adept, and skilled at ongoing experimentation. Unconstrained by rigid boundaries, they will tap regional *hot spots* around the world—nodes of connectivity, talent, and infrastructure. Work will increasingly be done anywhere, anytime, rather than in fixed locations on 9-to-5 schedules. Companies will adopt flexible relationships and continually active connections to attract talented employees as well as loyal customers.

Significant new technologies and changes in societal behavior are the vanguards of change occurring within corporations, both large and small.

✓ **Technology that allows many people to share knowledge and ideas:** A broadly defined collection of Web-based communities and hosted services, such as social networking sites, wikis, and folksonomies, allow a new level of sharing among large numbers of users. These technologies, collectively called "Web 2.0," make

FIGURE 6-1

Next-generation enterprises: Shifting the business model

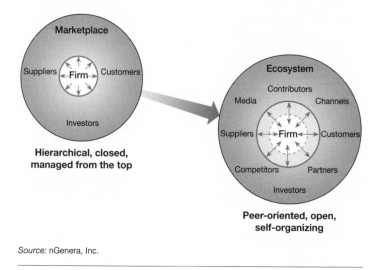

Source: nGenera, Inc.

---

it increasingly possible to collect, store, and employ conversations, wisdom, and know-how, allowing work to be
done in fundamentally different ways. Good ideas (including yours!) can spread quickly throughout a company;
challenges can be addressed through collective wisdom.

✓ **Advanced, easy-to-use search:** Search technology has
improved dramatically over the past few years. Before the
advanced algorithmic breakthroughs of Google, it was
hard to find what you were looking for. Using the Web
required significant skill. Today, thanks to Google and
others, people of all skill levels access information quickly
and easily.

✓ **Internet user sophistication:** As recently as the late 1990s, most adults older than thirty-five weren't accustomed to operating online. They didn't trust e-commerce sites with their credit cards and hadn't figured out how to form online communities. Today, most adults of all ages are comfortable buying things over the Internet, participating in online communities, and accessing information. They will increasingly do so at work.

✓ **Widely available broadband connections:** As recently as five years ago, online access was spotty and slow in most places. Today, always-on broadband connections are becoming widespread for businesses and individuals, allowing greater opportunity for flexible, virtual work.

✓ **The ability to "rent" software:** We are all beginning to use highly sophisticated and expensive software packages quickly and inexpensively. Think of the photography sites that allow you to edit your photos online, using the Web site's software rather than an expensive application installed on your computer. For corporations, this concept, called "software as a service," or SaaS, will virtually eliminate what has been a major barrier to agility and experimentation, by changing massive, time-consuming "buy" options into rapid, experimental "rent" approaches.

Technology is altering the landscape. It's no surprise, then, that change is afoot and is evident in a variety of new work relationships.

new relationships between corporations and those who perform work

Many corporations have some form of flex work policies on the books, but the current state of practice is mixed. Cultural taboos and prevailing management attitudes often dampen employees' willingness to take what is still perceived by many as a career risk. Nevertheless, you should expect to see a widening variety of relationships between employers and employees. Progressive companies are beginning to get serious about forming new relationships with those who perform work ("employees" may soon become a specialized subset of these relationships).

The most common options represent variations in time and place: flexible time, including individualized work schedules, flexible shifts, and compressed workweeks; reduced-time options, including a variety of part-time work, job sharing, and leaves of absence; and flexible workplaces, including telecommuting (working primarily from home) and mobile work (such as a salesperson who works mainly on the road).

Two other emerging options are cyclic work and "task, not time."

✓ **Cyclic work:** Over the next several decades, there will be a rapid increase in the number of people who work in cyclical—project-based—arrangements, many with no fixed affiliation to one corporation. This pattern allows individuals to work hard for a period of time and then move on to another work period, with the same or a new employer, or to periods of leisure or learning. Project-based work may even become the norm, each company having a small core of full-time employees (supplemented by a broad network of alliances) and most workers assembled by project as needed (think of the movie industry, where a producer assembles a unique cast and crew for each film).

✓ **Task, not time:** One of the most exciting options looming on the work horizon is the switch to task-based rather than time-based work arrangements. In this approach, employees are assigned specific tasks and required to put in only as much time as it actually takes to get the work done. This practice removes the need to keep regular hours or to show up at the office each day. It allows people to work asynchronously, instead of in standard 9-to-5 routines, and from virtually any location. This arrangement is very appealing to many Y's, who are used to the schoolwork model—doing your homework at your own speed rather than being held hostage in the library for a fixed number of hours. For many, the idea of staying in the office even after all your work is finished is annoying.

Practical realities in the economy encourage moving toward a task-based definition of jobs. It is difficult to quantify the time required for knowledge work: who can say how long it takes to, say, write a piece of software? And, with telecommuting and flexible hours, companies are essentially trusting that the task will be accomplished, although in most cases they still describe the job in terms of an expected number of hours.

As new ways of working become more widespread, corporations will be more attractive places for Y's to work. If the available work arrangements don't include the ones you'd prefer, encourage the creation of a wider variety. (My coauthors and I discussed many of these types of arrangements in our book *Workforce Crisis*.[2] Give the executives in your firm a copy!)

If you're headed into the corporate world, look for organizations that are open to change. And work with corporations to help them make the transition.

entrepreneurial and start-up options: facing better odds

A number of you already have a business on the side or a business plan in the works. One in four of you say you want to be an entrepreneur or own your own company. And for good reason: individuals who are self-employed are considerably more satisfied with their jobs than are other workers. They're more satisfied with their salaries, job security, chances for promotion, level of on-the-job stress, flexibility of hours, and proximity of work and home.[3]

Happily, the odds of success if you choose this path are improving—a little. Changes in the nature of work will open new doors for entrepreneurs: smaller, niche-focused firms, businesses built on offering greater personalization or individualization, and business models based on shared or collectively created information. New technologies reduce the advantages of scale and the costs of transactions, making it easier for small players to jump into the market. Smaller firms, specializing in core competencies, will proliferate.

We may, in fact, be entering a golden age for the small entrepreneur. Thomas W. Malone, a professor at the Massachusetts Institute of Technology, estimates that the Internet and powerful new off-the-shelf technologies have created an environment in which one out of ten small businesses will succeed, a much higher proportion than in the past.[4]

Sound good? What do you need to consider if you want to be an entrepreneur?

To begin with, even if Professor Malone's forecasts are correct, that still leaves a 90 percent failure rate. Choosing this option means choosing to risk great disappointment. By definition, these enterprises have, as older generations might say, all their eggs in one basket. That basket had better be a good one. For you, these businesses can represent a great roller-coaster ride—big ups, and possibly gut-wrenching downs. You have to be prepared for that. Of Gen Y's who have chosen to go the entrepreneurial route, 72 percent say they like to take risks.[5]

Second, long hours are often inescapable. Two-thirds of Gen Y entrepreneurs say they put in ten or more hours a day. Most of them conduct some type of business activity six out of seven days. Thirty-six percent of Generation Y business owners say they find it very difficult to leave their work to go on vacation.

And, of course, you need a good idea. To quote Sir Godfrey Hounsfield, inventor of computer-aided tomography (the CT scan), "Problems, problems! I've got to have problems!"[6] The best way to come up with a great business idea is to observe—and solve—a real problem. Most successful entrepreneurs draw their ideas from personal experience. A study of the five hundred fastest-growing U.S. companies found that 57 percent of the founders got the idea by seeing problems in the industry they had worked in before founding the company.[7] Ideas may also emerge from your experiences as a consumer—a product or service you've been dissatisfied with that you could address more effectively.

If you want to succeed, you'll need several personal characteristics. Most researchers agree that there is no neat set of behavioral attributes that describes an entrepreneurial personality, but it appears that entrepreneurs have a higher desire to be in control of their own fates. Independence is a key driver. Comfort with networking and marshaling resources is another key skill. Don't choose this route if you're shy about reaching out to others. Many Y's go into business with friends or family—people they trust and with whom they know they can collaborate.

Clearly there's satisfaction to be found in entrepreneurial options. Of Gen Y entrepreneurs, 75 percent say that having fun is a priority in the business, and 76 percent are certain that the decision they made to go into business was the right one. And 59 percent plan to be "serial" entrepreneurs, owning or planning to own more than one business—experimenting again and again.[8]

These Y's are beating the odds.

professional services: rethinking the one-size-fits-all career model

Professional services—including accounting, law, medicine, advertising, banking, consulting, and technology services—have long represented attractive career options for many people. Separating out educational services for a discussion that follows based on its somewhat different characteristics and challenges, these other professional services broadly offer higher-than-average compensation opportunities and, in the view of most people, significant prestige.

The good news about these places is that they really need top talent—their business models depend on having the best and the brightest on staff. As a result, firms tend to be leaders in innovative employment practices. Many are paving the way with new and creative forms of flexibility and performance management. Many are also leaders in the average levels of compensation they provide. In general, they offer extraordinary learning opportunities for those starting out in careers—chances to deal with a broad range of issues and to learn from accomplished senior colleagues. And the high-pressure atmosphere can provide a nearly addictive level of excitement for those who love to work that way.

Of course, there's a trade-off: most firms operate like the old apprentice system; you have to earn your stripes. Most professional service firms have a pyramid-shaped business model, featuring a significant number of junior staff members, a medium number of midcareer project managers, and a small number of senior leaders or partners at the top. Young hires typically work long hours, much of the time doing basic preparatory work for senior members, navigating a well-defined path of promotions up the pyramid, and, eventually, gaining an attractive share of the partnership profits.

At least that's the way it has worked for the past several decades. Today, these professions are facing a challenge in hiring; many of you are not very interested in investing days and weeks—much less years—of your life doing work that you view as boring and in itself unrewarding, in exchange for the distant hope of partnership.

As the pressures mount from Gen Y's and others seeking increasing flexibility, many professional service firms are beginning to offer a variety of career path options, recognizing that individuals go through life stages that may require different levels of work intensity—times when travel is difficult, weekends impossible, or other constraints on the profession's "always-on" ways of working come into effect. For example, accounting firm Deloitte has developed an approach it calls "mass career customization," which is designed to match people's assignments with their current life stage needs. Each individual's profile in the staffing database includes not only his or her skills and capabilities but also a variety of workstyle-related preferences and constraints.

education: challenging itself to meet twenty-first-century needs

Careers in education represent the opportunity to make a significant and immediate impact. The profession offers a certain degree of autonomy, the ability to exercise your creativity and put your own stamp on your day-to-day activities. Although the financial upside is more limited than that of some other options, it's a place that is proving popular with many Gen Y's.

It's also a place that is challenged to change—to strive for outcomes that are better matched to this century's job market. Education is reaching a crossroads. Over the next decade, I believe we will engage in a debate about the best ways to re-shape our approaches to education to ensure its relevance, both to the lives of people and the needs of businesses. You will be important contributors to this discussion and your creativity will help shape the ultimate solution.

nonprofits and social entrepreneurship: doing good—well

Both the traditional nonprofit world and the newly emerging sphere of social entrepreneurship require that you bring a strong value proposition to the table. Unlike large corporations that are designed to provide you with the resources to learn, many nonprofit organizations have little *free board*—that is, they have a limited capacity to invest in you. You need to be able to contribute early on.

Social entrepreneurship uses innovative, capitalist business models in the service of social needs. Traditional nonprofits increasingly apply top-quality business and management skills to the task at hand. The challenge for these organizations is to create extraordinary value using limited resources. The challenge for you, as you consider a career in this arena, is to understand the real value of the contribution you can make.

Classic not-for-profit organizations cover a broad gamut of activities and desired outcomes: social services, religion, education, the arts, and a number of others. For most such organizations, obtaining funding is often a more consuming aspect of their activities than is dispensing the benefits. The core of a successful nonprofit model involves having a strong commitment to and comfort with soliciting funding, combined with a highly efficient and effective method of providing service.

Social entrepreneurship's goals are aligned with those of non-profits: helping improve the lives of others. However, the approach is fundamentally different. Social entrepreneurship uses the principles of traditional profit-making business enterprise as the driving force for creating change. For example, some of the best-known models involve working with artisans in developing countries to provide them with access to global markets for their goods and, through this process, help them bring more money into the local economy.

Personal success in the world of nonprofits and social entrepreneurship requires much more than passion. Increasingly, these organizations are looking for people with substantive business skills to enable them to fulfill their mandates in efficient ways—to do what they do well. You need to have skills relevant to the operational model you are executing. For example, to distribute medicine to third world areas or relief supplies to disaster areas effectively, you would need a strong understanding of modern supply-chain techniques.

Many of you have the desire to make a difference. I know it sounds corny, but the combination of your sheer numbers—the size of your generation—and your caring attitudes will, I expect, allow you to affect many of the troubling issues in the world. Already organizations such as the Peace Corps and Teach for America rank among the most popular first career choices for Gen Y's.[9]

But make sure you're up to the challenge—and that you leverage your Generation Y strengths: maintain the integrity of your principles; be persistent; be passionate; be creative; make it fun. And make a difference.

the trades and other middle-skill jobs: not going away

Contrary to popular headlines, jobs requiring medium levels of educational training—perhaps a two-year associate degree—still exist in significant numbers. Although these jobs are becoming a smaller proportion of total employment—falling during the past two decades from 55 percent of all jobs in the United States to 48 percent—they still represent *almost half* of all employment opportunities.[10] Some of the fast-growing jobs in this category include computer support specialists, carpenters, electricians, plumbers, dental hygienists, laboratory technicians, mechanics, truck drivers, and paralegals.

Many of these jobs have experienced significant wage increases, based on tightening supply relative to demand. For example, real pay for radiological technicians increased 23 percent between 1997 and 2005, and for electricians, 18 percent. In contrast, the overall average increase for U.S. workers during the same period was 5 percent.

Many of these jobs also offer great opportunities for those of you who prefer work that creates something tangible or who value independence and flexibility. For example, many health care jobs now offer scheduling options in which you can work a full-time schedule in only three days. And, interestingly, these jobs are among the least likely to be subject to global labor competition—since many of them have to be done "here."

government service: offering unprecedented opportunity

The potential for immediate impact and long-term security makes government service careers attractive to many Y's. The downsides can include limited financial upside and a perceived need to negotiate through fairly rigid bureaucracies in many instances. However, because government service was a popular choice for the Boomer generation, many of whom are now planning to retire, there are numerous openings available and significant open air on your way to the top.

In a recent survey of U.S. college graduates the top ten most desirable employers included the U.S. Department of State, the Central Intelligence Agency, NASA, and the U.S. Department of Defense. In fact, a full 34 percent of you aged eighteen to twenty-nine expressed an interest in working for the federal government.[11]

This is very good news for the government. Predictions are dire when it comes to the future of the current federal workforce, and very good for those entering the workforce. According to experts, 60 percent of the federal government's General Schedule (rank-and-file) employees—and 90 percent of the Senior Executive Service (the federal government's top managers)—will be eligible to retire in the next ten years. The United States risks losing a huge portion of its experienced staff and the associated continuity, technical expertise, and institutional knowledge.

For those willing to work through the system, government service is yet another way Y's can do something significant.

. . . . .

Each of these places offers different pros and cons as you think about your career. In the next chapter, I talk about how to pull all the pieces together—how to make the trade-offs and align the reality of your needs and preferences to zero in on work that will work for you.

7. align the practical realities

So far, I've encouraged you to consider a broad range of possibilities and search for work that you will love. Now, it's time to home in—to consider the practical realities of your specific situation and the down-to-earth needs you may have for a job. In this chapter, I look at considerations such as the amount of money you need to make, the time you're interested in devoting to work, and the level of responsibility you're willing to assume. If they don't align with your biggest dreams, you may need to prioritize your wants and needs and decide which concessions to make as you start your career.

This chapter is about the practical reality that works for you (and your partner and family)—what you are willing to invest in terms of time, energy, and money in the deal and what you need and want in return.

For example, suppose you have concluded thus far that your archetype is expressive legacy and your passion is writing books. After evaluating the practical considerations raised in this chapter, you may conclude that your current economic reality includes a heavy student debt load and family commitments that call for significant financial stability for the immediate future. In this example, then, you might decide that you will need to compromise at least for a while; rather than go immediately for your ultimate dream, it may be better to look for a job that carries a little less financial risk but that hopefully will still suit your expressive legacy work preference.

Here, I offer a framework for organizing your thoughts on the practical realities you face, and I also share two stories of Gen Y's who are in the midst of wrestling with these trade-offs.

Let's begin with Dan. His story is about both a journey to find what he really loves doing and the practical realities that nudged him in different directions along the way. It is illustrative of the Gen Y career path I have been describing—several different starts to find the one that fits best, but all based on pursuing passion—but now marrying passionate interests to practical concerns.

dan's story: practical expression of life's passion

When we spoke, Dan was deep into his job search.[1] With college graduation looming only a few months away, he had been thinking hard about the "what next" question and was coming out in a place that neither he nor his friends might have expected four years earlier.

Dan has always been passionate about music. In high school, he played the piano, composed music, and developed his knack for organizing things by founding a concert series. He took a gap year after high school, working for City Year, an organization in which young people work as tutors and mentors, running after-school programs and leading youth leadership programs. His role there as operations director for large-scale service days further developed his capabilities for organization and business productivity. As he says, "On the heels of City Year, I was more confident as an organizer than as an artist."

In college, Dan continued to explore the link between his love of music and his skill in running things. In the spring of his freshman year in college, Dan joined the founding team of an independent record label associated with a musician who had been one of Dan's favorites growing up. "I'd always wanted to produce—working in a studio, being part of the writing and recording process," he says.

After a year of not doing any of his own music, Dan felt that he had lost his edge as a performer: "I knew that I was now a small fish in a big pond." But as a member of the Songwriters and Performers Society (SAPS) at NYU, Dan had the opportunity to meet lots of musicians, becoming good friends with a few. "I was witnessing the potential of a few of my friends. We'd get together for coffee once a week, and I turned into a sort of career counselor. As a songwriter/producer, I could empathize with them as artists." At the same time, Dan was becoming disillusioned with the values of others at the record label, and eventually he decided to leave.

Dan wanted to start his own management company, build-ing on the network he'd established in the music community. From June to December 2005, he was a go-getter, laying the groundwork for his entrepreneurial venture—filing a business certificate, starting a bank account, and launching a Web site. He went on a tour with one artist and recorded a successful full-length album with another. Things were going very well.

Then in December of his sophomore year, Dan saw the movie *Brokeback Mountain*. Although he'd been openly gay since high school, he found that watching the film and reading the story were deeply personal experiences. As he talked about the film with friends, he started to see it as a story of escapism. The every-day lives of the two men seemed superficial, an act, but the moun-tain itself was real—it symbolized not only their love for each other but also of each man for himself. Dan realized that the film had hit "a nerve of loneliness within me"—a strong desire to get back to doing things that were more authentically "him."

As he got deeper into his work as a manager, Dan felt increas-ingly disconnected from himself. He wasn't writing—fulfilling his own emotional needs. Instead, he was doing promotional and administrative work for other writers. He remembers thinking that he had once known the feeling of being "on the moun-tain" but was no longer sure where or when it was. "I wanted to rediscover that feeling."

The event that galvanized him was attending a huge inde-pendent media conference. From Dan's perspective, every panel might as well have been called, "How Do I Generate Cash Flow?" Folks who were once focused on the art were now scrambling to provide for themselves and, even worse, their families. Dan's conversations with the people he met there were disappointing. He found himself missing the kind of intellectual challenge that he had enjoyed during high school English classes or while writing music.

On his flight home from the conference, Dan reflected on the mottos of schools he'd attended and organizations he had worked with:

✓ Honesty, Compassion, Respect

✓ Work Conquers All

✓ Virtue Always Green (or Fresh/Alive)

✓ Putting Idealism to Work

His conclusion was simple: those values *were* important to him, and they wouldn't work in the music business he'd come to know. He needed to find a career in which he wouldn't have to sacrifice his values—and one in which his sense of self, his "mountain," would be something he would be living daily.

The idea of teaching had always lingered in his mind. Dan credited his high school experience at a top boarding school as a major influence on his teen years. Boarding school "provided a community in which I could be myself and discover myself." Everyone on campus knew that he was gay, but they "saw me as a musician, newspaper writer, ropes course instructor, and good student." Dan had built close, long-term friendships and strong relationships with his teachers.

As he thought about a career in teaching, he realized he felt excited by the idea of serving as a role model—as someone who didn't narrow his life—to students from different backgrounds. He was also attracted by the diversity and tolerance that are typical in such environments. As he says, "I've felt torn between two worlds. I'm gay but don't feel comfortable in the gay scene. In straight culture, I often feel like the exception. I love hip-hop, but also folk music. It's hard to find friends who will dance to one, but also drink beers to another." He wanted to be part of a diverse community.

Dan got back to New York, closed the recording company, enrolled in summer courses, and dove in to study the classics and Latin. He reveled in the feeling of moving forward and returning all at once. Returning to the goal of teaching—one that had been overshadowed by his musical ambitions—heightened his understanding of his own experience as a student. He connected his "mountain" to life in an intellectually rigorous boarding school.

He is passionate about sharing his love of the subjects he will teach. "I want to be a part of students seeing the deep connection between language and self-expression. Language and art are our best attempts as humans to express the elusive quality of our experiences. Greek and Latin capture this beautifully in their poetry. Words have feelings and relationships to each other. Words matter."

Dan's also looking forward to teaching skills such as grammar. He says of this passion, "I'm a complete nerd for these sorts of skills. In college, I met *many* students who didn't understand grammar at all. The idea of language disintegrating is just terrible."

Long term, Dan has different ideas about where his career might go, but his priorities for right now are as follows:

✓ "Location—being near the city that is a hub for my family. But not *in* the city, just near. I'm done with city life for now."

✓ "Living in a tolerant community. Massachusetts allows gay marriage/adoption, so that majorly figures into my geographical preference."

✓ "Working in a place that will provide a lot of support for me as a new teacher. I want a school to empower me rather than just throw me into a classroom."

✓ "Being able to teach multiple subjects. I want to teach English primarily but would love to teach Latin as well. I look forward to coaching."

✓ "Earning money insomuch as I feel valued by my employer. However, I'd rather balance my life due to financial constraints rather than indulge my life with wealth."

✓ "Having the opportunity to earn my master's degree in English—either subsidized by my employer or rewarded by an increased salary."

✓ "Owning a cabin in Montana, not an estate."

✓ "Taking the summers off!"

Dan has concluded that "while I have many career goals for the long term, the overarching life goal is to, as Joseph Campbell put it, 'follow my bliss.' How corny?! I know . . . Living and working in a balanced community in which I can integrate physical health and creativity might help to balance my own self." And as he notes, the journey is not over: "Who knows how I will feel about life and my career in a year, two years, five years?"

the practical reality: your carillon curves

Strategy, in essence, is a choice or a series of choices. For a company, having a strategy implies that its management has a consistent and logical basis for determining where and how to invest the organization's resources, both time and money. The implication for a career strategy is no different. To shape one, you need a basis for choosing where to invest your time, energy, and perhaps money.

your career curve

What shape will your career take? The line of your career is not an even progression. The amount of time, the intensity of your involvement with the work, the pulls of family, and many other concerns influence the shape at any given moment of that path—what I call the *career curve.*

The career curve framework guides you in thinking about the practical reality of what will work for you (and your partner and family). How much money do you consider enough (or need so that you can pay off the debt that you are carrying from school loans)? How much time would you like to devote to work? What role would you like it to play in the mosaic of your life's other activities?

Older adults have tended to think about one career curve. It used to be that the progression of a career meant a steady rise at one workplace through the years, and then a sharp and abrupt end—rather like falling off a cliff—when workers retired. That pattern is being replaced, by and large, by more of a bell curve: entry-level, full involvement and advancement, and then a winding down or deceleration phase as workers transition out of work. Gen Y's, however, should be thinking of multiple curves. Quite likely, like Dan, you will have ups, downs, and do-overs. For you, the career curve framework might better be called *career carillon*, because the line of your career is likely to resemble a series of bell curves (see figure 7-1).[2]

As you think about the options for your career curve(s), consider these issues.

- ✓ **Time:** What other priorities do you have for your life? How much time would you like to devote to work? On the surface, this question is probably the most straightforward of all the considerations, although it's also one of the most dependent on other choices you make. To a large extent, the amount of time you choose to devote to various activities, including work, will end up depending on how much you enjoy each one relative to the others. Nonetheless, it's important to consider that, realistically, some careers are far more time-consuming than others.

FIGURE 7-1

Career Carillon

Your career is likely to be a series of bell curves.

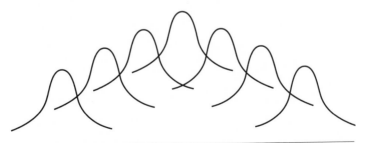

✓ **Rhythm:** Lots of people say they'd like more flexibility in their work arrangements, but what would that really mean for you? How much spontaneity or predictability do you need to accomplish the other priorities in your life? Do you anticipate having other activities that are highly regular (for example, training for an athletic event that could be conducted at the same time every day), or are your other priorities more likely to be spontaneous (for example, going on an impromptu trip)? Would working four long days every week—the same four days—be more appealing to you, or would you rather work in episodic bursts? Various career choices allow various rhythms.

✓ **Economic reality:** Get out your pencil or spreadsheet. It's time to set some approximate financial goals. How much money do you need at this stage of your life? What standard of living will be comfortable for you? This is not a book about financial planning—there are plenty of those—but I encourage you to do some now. Be sure to take into account not only living expenses but also money required to pay off any student loans and to save for dreams you may have for the future. Consider the amount of help that you can realistically expect from your parents and family. Having a rough sense of your economic requirements will shape the choices that make sense.

✓ **Challenge:** Consider the extent to which you want (or don't want) to take on difficult or challenging roles at this point, including the level of commitment you would be willing to make to learn new skills and capabilities. How new and how difficult do you want your future work to be?

✓ **Responsibility:** Responsibility is a measure of the interdependence of your work with that of others. How willing are you to take on roles, including managerial tasks, that directly affect others? Are you comfortable having others depend on you? Are you willing to have people look to you for leadership or direction?

These questions help you shape the tangible reality of the work you prefer. Time and money may not be all that counts, but they are an important reality to factor in as you search for your passion.

career curve archetypes

The most likely combinations of career curve considerations create several familiar archetypes (see table 7-1). See whether these capture the relationship you'd like to have with work. Better yet, develop your own unique profile.

✓ **Intellectual:** You like to work in intense bursts, with flexibility and challenge.

✓ **Customer-facing:** You enjoy interacting with others in roles that are relatively straightforward, well defined, and service oriented.

✓ **Behind the scenes:** You love work that is predictable, clearly scheduled, and could be done on a part-time basis.

TABLE 7-1

Career Curve: Common archetypes

	Intellectual	Customer-facing	Behind the scenes	Interdependent	Change agent	Entrepreneur
Time	M–H	L–M	L–M	H	L–H	H+
Rhythm	F	F	P	P	F	F
Economic requirements	M–H	L–M	L–M	H	L	L
Challenge	H	L	L	H	M–H	H
Responsibility	L	L	L	H	M–H	H
Possible work options	Project contractor	Retail	Customer service	Managerial	Charitable	Start-up
	Consultant	Technical support				

H, M, L = High, Medium, Low
F, P = Flexible, Predictable

✓ **Interdependent:** You enjoy being in the center of a complex team of people and are willing to assume intense roles.

✓ **Change agent:** You like to take on significant challenges and have relatively low needs for additional income.

✓ **Entrepreneur:** You are willing to invest significant amounts of time, and perhaps money, to tackle big challenges.

There is no no-risk option. But you can create a life suited to your strengths and passions—and balanced with the practical realities—if you take advantage of the opportunities all around and if you're not afraid to close the door on one path and begin another when necessary.

allison's story: practical trade-offs to meet multiple priorities

Allison Blood is highly organized and *very* busy.[3] A senior in college, Allison is a nursing student with a business minor. She is also passionate about horses. She trains young horses, teaches riding, and competes. In between, she runs a major program for the local riding organization and does a variety of other volunteer work.

Allison's life plans reflect the thoughtful consideration she brings to most aspects of her life. Although she grew up on a farm, she never considered making a career in the horse world. She knows how tough and uncertain the horse business can be. And farm life wasn't an option either. Allison wants something that offers security, stability, and insurance.

Allison's love of animals and science initially led her to consider a career as a veterinarian. However, she recognized that the round-the-clock demands of that career would leave her little time to enjoy her own horses and, later, the family she plans to have. She considered becoming a doctor, but the investment of time and money required to go to school for all those years was a drawback.

She chose nursing as the best blend of these practical considerations. Nursing allows her to work in a field she loves and in an occupation that offers flexible scheduling options. For example, it's possible to work three twelve-hour shifts a week and be considered full-time. Some nurses with younger children work part-time: two twelve-hour shifts.

After one year's experience in a hospital, it is possible to create even greater flexibility. Many nurses elect to sign on with a nursing agency. This option offers cyclic work (as discussed in chapter 6). Allison knows colleagues who have been at the same hospital for many years, but on an agency basis. These nurses work three months, then take time off, and then sign back on for another three months.

In addition to flexible hours, nursing faces a significant shortage of available staff and, as a result, offers attractive financial incentives. One package Allison is considering includes $10,000 per year to pay off loans. Most offer attractive benefits: dental and health insurance, public transportation passes, free on-site parking, and even gym memberships for the employee and her family. As Allison wisely notes, "The little things add up."

Nursing will provide the money she needs to have a life that includes horses.

After several years, Allison plans to begin studying to get her master's degree, taking advantage of the hospital's willingness to contribute to her tuition per year. With a master's, she will become a nurse practitioner, eligible for even more attractive compensation.

Nursing also offers flexibility of place. Allison will be able to choose a facility that balances access to challenging cases and proximity to rural areas, so it will be easy for her to get to a place where she can ride and teach.

For Allison, nursing seems like an optimum trade-off of money, time to degree, and ultimate flexibility. And it's one she is sure she loves. Her hands-on experience with horses creates a strong set of caretaking skills. Having been committed to community service throughout her life, she loves the service aspect of the profession: "It's part of what pushed me toward being a nurse or doctor."

She would like to get married and have children at some point—no earlier than age thirty. Once she has children, she plans to cut back the amount of time she works, again using the flexibility of her chosen profession to balance her life. Her expectation is that she will work only one or two shifts per week, only when her husband is home to stay with the children.

Allison credits her parents, and particularly her father, with giving her persistence and an appreciation of hard work, of doing chores and taking care of your equipment, and of doing a thorough job in the amount of time you have. She wants to let her children have the same experience growing up that she had—the responsibility of work and the fun of horses and the farm. She has mapped out a practical path that will allow her to pursue multiple passions—medicine, horses, and family.

the process of discovery

The questions posed in this and earlier chapters are not analytical frameworks that will lead you to one answer, but rather what I like to think of as prisms that let the light shine through. Hold up each option you consider against these frameworks to see how each looks against your practical reality.

We know, from sound research, that adults find their way forward by trying new things, evaluating each one as they go—continually searching for the path that works best for them. As expressed by Herminia Ibarra, a professor of organizational behavior at INSEAD, "Identities change in practice, as we start doing new things (*crafting experiments*), interacting with different people (*shifting connections*), and reinterpreting our life stories through the lens of the emerging possibilities (*making sense*)."[4]

Viewing each possibility through the lens of your personal criteria is one way of making sense.

. . . . .

In chapter 8, we look at questions to ask and signals to be on the lookout for as you search for the right position.

8. find the perfect job

I've talked about things to consider when you're choosing an overall career direction—what you love, what you prefer, the place where you're likely to find those, and the practical realities of what you are prepared to take on in time and money. Now you have another set of choices. Now, let's find your perfect job![1]

When you select a *specific* job, you are committing to four things:

✓ The location where you will live

✓ The company you will be associated with—its practices, policies, and reputation

✓ The colleagues you will work with day-to-day, particularly your boss

✓ The actual assignment you will be performing

Let's begin the search.

location, location, location: choosing where you live

Three out of four Americans under the age of twenty-eight say that a cool community is more important than a good job. Two-thirds of college-educated twenty-five- to thirty-four-year-olds say they will first decide where to live and *then* will look for work. In the United Kingdom, job seekers aren't after the positions that will net them the most money. Instead, their top priority is location (47 percent).[2]

From your perspective, what makes for a great location? Here are some of the types of things that many Y's say are important.

✓ **Porosity:** Is it possible to "get in" to the community? Some places are much more receptive to newcomers than others. Is the community you are considering run by the same few people who have always run it? Are they looking for new blood, or do they like it the way it is? Chances are you don't want to live in a place where, after nearly ten years, people still consider you new to town!

✓ **Public spaces:** Are there places and spaces for social interactions—areas where you can be out and about, such as coffeehouses, streets that are friendly for walking, and parks? Is the quality of life in these spaces high—are they clean, attractive, safe, and green? Where do the people of the community spend their time when not at work? If the answer is "almost always in their homes," it will be hard to feel connected to the community. Starbucks has used the phrase "third place" to describe the increasingly important space that is neither home nor work where people can meet and hang out.

✓ **Professional:** Will it be possible to meet your ongoing professional and economic aspirations in this city? Are there growth opportunities, multiple employers, places for learning?

✓ **People:** What are the chances that you will come in contact with people you enjoy being with in this community? How easy will it be to make connections? Are the people interesting and diverse? How close is this place to your family?

For many Y's, the last criterion—being close to family—trumps all other location considerations.

By the way, the importance of location to Y's has not been lost on potential employers or communities. You represent a popular target for city planners; individuals between the ages of twenty-five and thirty-four are considered the dream demographic of a fast-growing economy.

finding the right company

Finding a company you feel good about is an essential step. Even if you're on a career path that you love, the company you're with can make or break the entire deal. Even with the best assignments and terrific colleagues, you won't have a great job if the company's policies and practices get in the way.

The reasons given by young employees for preferring one company over another run a wide gamut. Culture, learning opportunities, team-based work environments, fancy amenities, and time off are only some of the reasons that companies have made it to lists of top employers.

Later in this chapter I discuss the nature of assignments given to new employees. For now, let's turn to some of the other features you'll want to consider.

learning opportunities

Strong learning environments are one of the major reasons that companies are listed among the "Best Places to Launch a Career" in *BusinessWeek*'s annual survey of career counselors, employers, and Gen Y's.[3] One of your most important objectives in assessing new work opportunities should be to discover whether the organization is committed to building your knowledge, expertise, and reputation. Look for companies that offer strong leadership programs, respected in-house training capabilities, and significant financial commitments to development. After you've asked whether there is an investment in learning, check out the *type* of learning. Look for clear evidence of the following.

✓ **On-the-job learning experiences:** Look at whether other recent hires are doing work they find challenging and whether other workers freely share what they know.

✓ **Executives who create a "gift culture":** Ask your interviewers to talk about the executives' involvement in informal mentoring. Is it the norm that leaders provide lots of feedback, career advice, and frequent coaching?[4]

✓ **Formal development programs:** These include a variety of learning approaches (classroom, online, coaching, mentoring), all clearly communicated and easily accessible.

culture

The term *corporate culture* covers a broad range of characteristics and can be one of the hardest aspects of a job for you to gauge going in—and one of the most de-

> –**The company invests in people and makes an effort to provide opportunities for new roles . . . This sends the message that people are of value.**

moralizing if you find yourself in a corporate culture you really don't like. There are a lot of positives that may initially catch your eye.

✓ **A sense of creativity:** For example, Disney is known for an unabashed sense of creativity, optimism, and decency; Google, for the policy of letting all employees devote one day a week to developing new ideas.

✓ **A spirit of collaboration and commitment to team players:** For example, the extensive interview process at Goldman Sachs is designed largely to judge candidates' potential fit with the existing team.

✓ **Special amenities:** Abbott Laboratories offers on-site fitness centers and a "sports and activities" program. Google provides free gourmet lunches and on-site massages.

Even with these kinds of eye-catching extras, frustration with basic work practices is among the greatest complaints of Y's after they've spent a year or two in the corporate world. For many Y's already in the workplace, the cultural issues they wish they'd probed more closely before joining their current firms

–In general, things move way too slowly.

–I didn't see how bureaucratic it is. Our generation wants to do it now—not, "Can you approve this?"

are ones related to *how work actually gets done*—the availability and use of current technology, the rigidity of the hierarchy, the way individuals are expected to spend their time, and, in general, what might be termed "bureaucracy." Red tape is a major barrier to Y's constant desire for speed in getting work done and decisions made, and it's a key determinant of whether or not they enjoy the culture.

To avoid getting stuck in a slow-moving culture, ask questions and observe clues such as the ones I discuss next.

APPROVALS PROCESSES. Ask questions like, "What would the process be like to get one of my recommendations implemented?" Ask your interviewers to walk you through specific examples of the decisions you will need to have made to get

–Gen X is really big on meetings—while I could have had a fifteen-minute call with my group. Instead I come out of a long meeting and feel burned out . . . and still have to do my job!

–We don't need all the meetings. Just give us the information!

your work done and how that is likely to occur. Understanding the number of people involved and the nature of the process will give you more insight than just asking whether the culture is bureaucratic.

MEETINGS. Ask people how much time they've spent in meetings and for what purposes. Are the meetings just "show-and-tell," or are they working sessions, full of engaged discussion and opportunity for collaboration?

TECHNOLOGY. Most of you have high expectations for the technology you will use at work, but, because many companies are not as up to speed as you are, you may find old technology getting in the way of speed and effectiveness. Ask about the types of technology that will be available to you and about how technology is leveraged in the business. Watch how older colleagues are using technology. It can be frustrating to some of you if other employees are not comfortable using the technologies you're adept at.

If you find a mismatch, consider that it may not be a deal-killer. You may be able to influence change. In fact, maybe you're being recruited specifically to bring new perspectives, so don't necessarily be discouraged by what you find. But do ask (polite) questions about the company's openness to trying new approaches. One that is supportive of your initiatives in this area will give you room to grow (and grow the culture, too).

–I got my own software through IT. I'm the only person in the unit who is using the software. Everyone is reaping the benefits of what I've learned and the reports I can run.

If your position will involve working remotely, inquire about the technology support you'll have. Y's are three times as likely as others to work off-site and, as a result, depend on technology for the necessary connections.[5]

COMMUNICATION AND INFORMATION SHARING. Depending on the nature of the work you'll be doing, you may need to access information from multiple sources. Ask whether the workplace uses collaborative tools, such as wikis, blogs, and social networking sites. Be alert to any restrictions or policies that the company may have that would prevent you from working in ways that you may be assuming will be possible.

practices related to time

Understanding the company's practices related to time management is another important element of whether a company ultimately works for you.

Some of the policies will be readily apparent and undoubtedly carefully explained during the interview process. For example, policies related to flex-time and place are becoming increasingly common. Vacation policy can vary widely and is something you're likely to hear about during the recruiting process. Take time to understand all of these: what is possible and when each option will be available to you (if it's not at the time of hire).

–Gen Y wants more of a work–life balance . . . Maybe we're just more efficient.

–Be more flexible with timing—if I work late one day, why can't I leave earlier the next day? I need some time for *life*.

And then there's the more straightforward issue of how many hours you are expected to put in. Be sure to ask questions to help you understand these important, and often unspoken, norms.

Think about time one other way: a *great* work environment will allow you to match the hours spent to those actually required to get the task done. The organization will recognize efficiency, measuring you on the tasks you do and not the hours you spend.

–We are all working more than we want to.

–Worst thing is the number of hours—sixty on average.

Not long ago, I spoke with the chief financial officer of a major New York–based corporation. Clearly frustrated, he explained that everyone in his department worked sixty or more hours a week. They always had, and, as far as he was concerned, they always would. But he was having no luck finding young employees willing to accept this schedule. "Everyone says that they're willing to work thirty-five hours a week, maybe forty in a pinch," he complained. "I need you to come in and talk to them."

"Well, I could do that," I responded, "but first, let me talk with you . . ."

I explained to the CFO that the Y's he was trying to recruit were probably amazed that older workers require so much time to get their work done. In general, Y's are happy to do the task required but are sure

–With so much technology, I feel like I should be able to work how I want, as long as I'm getting it done.

–Give me a task, and I'll come back to you with it when I'm done.

–Older generations still gauge the quality of work by the number of hours put into it.

it would take a *lot* less than sixty hours if all or most of the non-essential face-to-face interactions were eliminated.

A flexible organization will not only allow you to adjust your hours of coming and going, but also will recognize efficiency, measuring you on the tasks you do and not the hours you spend.

money

As I mentioned in chapter 3, Gen Y's views on money vary widely. For some of you, it is a crucial consideration as you choose a job. Others—in fact, 70 percent of you—say you would rather work for smaller growth companies that offer competitive benefits and emphasize a balance between work activities and your personal lives, than larger companies that may offer high salaries at the expense of longer, more rigid hours and less-exciting job assignments.[6] The key, of course, is to find a compensation package that matches your needs and priorities.

Consider not only the amount of money offered but also the breadth of rewards, including greater opportunities and formal recognition. Ask potential peers you meet about their

–There are other, higher-paying jobs, but location, work environment, and the actual work here is better.

–The opportunity to work abroad is a big reward.

feelings regarding the level and type of recognition they receive.

Of course, the money itself counts, and, at least in recent years, pay has been increasing at top firms as talent shortages grow. In 2006, only nine companies in the top fifty in the *BusinessWeek* "Best Places to Launch a Career" survey offered starting salaries of at least $55,000. In 2007, twice that many were offering big money, among them the brand-name tech companies.

Benefit packages are an important part of the overall package, too. Among Y's in the United States, medical and dental benefits and tuition reimbursement are most valued. And, particularly when it comes to complex benefit packages, you should make sure you are clear about what's being offered; many of you have not sorted through benefits options before.

–It's all about the money. Well, the schedule matters, too.

–If I could get paid more for doing the work, that would be a huge thing.

honest feedback

Most of you have high expectations for success at work: you are willing to work hard when it makes sense (to you), but you expect to see a goal and to understand the meaning and value of your work. You want feedback.

–I got a big book with words I didn't recognize, couldn't weed through, so I threw it aside.

–We didn't learn about money management in high school. Explain the benefits!

How does the organization you're considering evaluate and recognize performance? During the interview process, ask questions about the following:

✓ The frequency and formality of the feedback you can expect to receive; constructive criticism and *informal* reviews that point you in the right direction

✓ The criteria that will be used to measure your performance, including the amount of subjectivity built into the evaluation

✓ Other employees' perception of the fairness of the evaluation process

✓ The philosophy behind the evaluation system—is it a forced rating, so that some have to "lose" if others "win"?

✓ The organization's reputation for follow-up on any promises or suggestions made during the review

–My issue is forced ratings (1–5). In order to achieve excellent or outstanding, someone has to hit 3 . . . So there can't be a win/win.

–I'd rather my boss was more involved—was more aware of what I'm working on, and stepped in where needed to provide feedback, positive or negative.

Companies are beginning to pay more attention to developing performance management and feedback approaches that work well for Y's—in many cases, making feedback more frank, constructive, and direct. Boeing, for example, encourages managers to provide honest appraisals of new employees' work. The aerospace giant teaches managers how to deliver criticism—harsh, if necessary—along with praise.

career advice

Most of you want to know on the day you are hired how and where you can advance. You like career paths that include process clarity and options for high variety and personalization. What do you need to do to get to each level? What's the top level you can reach? To avoid disappointment with career path experiences, remember the importance of asking about each of the following before joining any organization:

✓ Rotational development programs, what I would call lateral career moves: the opportunity to take on new challenges by moving sideways in the organization when promotion slots are not available, as well as the frequency with which these moves are possible

–There is a two-year rule here, meaning that you need to stay in your job for two years before you can move. We don't like it. The two-year rule gets in the way of my ability to move into the job that I really want.

–I just wish I knew what I had to do . . . There's no career path, no career guide. What certification do I need? What client group do I need to support? It's just doing and hoping here.

✓ Opportunities for management and leadership training, including chances to hear from senior staff about their career experiences

✓ Regular, informal and formal development discussions with your manager or supervisor—conversations focused not on work that you have done, but rather on where you might go and how to get there

Top employers are working to meet Y's career path preferences.

✓ Abbott Laboratories recently began an extended orientation that includes goals for the first, second, and third months on the job, as well as the promise of consistent dialogue with managers.

✓ PricewaterhouseCoopers lets employees themselves decide when, during their first ninety days, they will sit down with their bosses for a performance review.

✓ KPMG has launched a Web-based training program to better prepare young employees and their managers to talk about career building. In the first two months, more than ninety-three hundred employees logged on. Some twenty-five hundred created their own (ideal) career paths.

first impressions

First impressions count—both the one you make and the one the company makes on you. In the case of the company, first impressions include the way it attracts your attention and provides initial information, as well as the process it uses for hiring and on-boarding.

You can learn a lot about a company by the way it reaches out to you. Does it use progressive approaches to attract candidates? Does it come across as open and honest about what it's like to work there, and do its practices reflect the way Y's operate? Look for rich Web sites that offer lots of information about the company, its history, what it does, and what the career opportunities are. It's important that employee testimonials, stories, and experiences be posted, too; you can use them to make sure that the image painted by the company recruiter of what it's like to work there is borne out in the comments of current and past employees. Top employers are beginning to use increasingly innovative, Y-oriented recruiting and retention practices, such as Facebook postings and videos—a sign that they are taking your interests and ways of communicating into their culture.

The way companies manage the hiring and on-boarding process will tell you a lot about how together they are and will give you important clues about the cultural norms. Companies that are sensitive to Gen Y:

✓ Don't drag out the hiring process

✓ Maintain communication with you throughout the process, by phone, text messaging, IM, e-mail, or mail—whatever you tell them is best for you

✓ Have a clear process for on-boarding and induction (which they describe to you before you take the job) that will help you understand how the company is structured, how to get things done, and whom to go to with ideas and suggestions as well as information, along with providing opportunities to meet other new hires early in the process

reputation and values you are proud to be associated with

Most of you want to plug in to a company that reflects your values. Start by learning everything possible about how the company is viewed by others. Look for both the absence of negatives and the presence of positives. You don't want to find that the company has, for example, environmental practices you aren't comfortable with, investments in activities that you don't support, or ethical lapses.

On the positive side, consider whether the company has a well-known brand name that will build your résumé through association, is known to have a culture that resonates with you, or supports philanthropic and community activities you care about.

Depending on your values, you may gravitate to corporations having various types of images. Stability and promotion from within are hallmarks of Raytheon. Commitment to social service is the core of Teach for America and the Peace Corps.

–I was attracted to join because I had a good experience as a customer.

–Reviews from past employees were good.

–It's never in the news for negative issues.

–It's known for having a family company and culture.

–It's known as a company that cares about employees.

choosing your colleagues

There's an old saying in business that individuals join a company but leave a boss. This means that even though you may be attracted to the policies and practices of a company—and they are important—in the end, the individual to whom you report may be the biggest influence on your ultimate job experience. In your job hunt you need to consider the boss and colleagues you'll be working with as much as you do the organization itself.

a boss who will bring out the best in you

Gen Y's expect attention from managers. You have experienced frequent feedback from parents, teachers, coaches, scout leaders, and other adults all your lives, so it's natural to expect a similar level of input, evaluation, and guidance at work. If you interview with the person who will be your immediate supervisor, look for someone who

A great manager is . . .

–Someone who listens to suggestions, and, even if the suggestions are not accepted, explains why.

–Someone who gives me a task, explains the context, and then leaves me alone to figure it out.

–Someone who lets me go—move on—after helping me get there.

seems genuinely interested in working with you, someone you feel you can learn from and whose style will give you room to grow.

In addition to forming your own impressions during the interview, try to request interviews with peers who also report to this individual. Ask them to talk about their day-to-day experience.

coworkers who are supportive and will help you learn

Evaluating your future coworkers is a valid and important part of the job search. What are the people like? Do you personally like them based on your interactions so far? Would you want to be friends with them? After all, you'll be spending a lot of time with these people.

Look for evidence of collaboration—people helping each other and sharing information—and for relationships among colleagues that seem supportive.

Don't be put off if many of your future coworkers are older than you. Many Y's find they have developed wonderful relationships with older colleagues at work. Not all have been so fortunate, but for those who have, the relationship can be one of mutual respect and tremendous learning.

–I can ask my older colleagues any question and depend on their experience.

–People who know what they are talking about—those are the ones I gravitate to. It's not based on rank.

–I'm always learning every day, and the guys are good at telling me what I need to pay attention to.

Many Y's have told us during our research that they really like working with Boomers. Mentoring relationships between Y's and Boomers appear to be valued and productive. One hitch: many of you seem to turn to Boomer colleagues preferentially, rather than to your direct managers, for advice or opportunities to learn new skills. This can run against the grain in some highly structured hierarchies and, taken to the extreme, can create conflicts with less-experienced Gen X bosses.

Of course, not all older coworkers are going to welcome you with open arms. Some may feel threatened by your way of doing things, be unwilling to share knowledge with a newcomer from another generation, or just be slow to welcome you into an established group. You don't necessarily need to cross the job off your list if you find this type of environment, but consider seriously how you will work with your new colleagues to create as favorable a win/win as possible.

–When someone says, "We should try to use this," some people will say no instantly—the generation gap comes up.

–I had to spend a lot of time winning their favor, demonstrating I could do the job. It is hard to come out of college and convince them I could pick up and do the same job.

assignments: the nature of the work

Finally, a very important part of your search for a great job is to evaluate the nature of the work itself, to find an assignment that fits your interests and lets you use and expand your skills. Assignments that are important, challenging, and visible are hugely attractive to Gen Y's. To understand what your initial experience will be like, be sure to ask enough questions.

responsibility

Y's value working on tasks that matter. You want to feel that you're doing something important during the time you spend at work.

The companies at the top of the "Best Places to Launch a Career" list recognize this and offer new employees positions that reflect this value. For example, the top three spots in 2007 were held by Deloitte & Touche, PricewaterhouseCoopers, and Ernst & Young because of, ironically, the visibility and importance taken on by the accounting profession in the wake of the Enron scandal. Accountants don't labor out of sight; they are vital to the fortunes of a company. Accounting provides Y's with an opportunity to be in an important position that's visible and responsible.

–I like the fact that the boss gives me a project and I can just handle it.

–My boss left, and I became the "go-to" guy after six months. Very cool.

Enterprise Rent-A-Car is known for offering new hires some of the most independent and entrepreneurial opportunities available. After a management training program that has been compared to an MBA crash course, new hires get to run their own business.

As you evaluate the specific assignments that you will be given initially, look for the degree to which they will provide you with responsibility.

challenge and contribution

Y's like to be challenged, and they chafe at what I call "prove it" jobs. As a result, companies are reshaping entry-level positions to provide significant opportunities.

✓ New York Life Insurance decided to get serious about using the talents of new hires. The company discontinued giving Friday afternoons off, ordered Y's into classes on business etiquette, and put them to work figuring out how to make the company's products more appealing to other Gen Y's.

✓ DHL, which usually hires only experienced salespeople, decided to offer an eleven-week program in sales to nine recent college grads. Pooja Shambhu, a twenty-four-year-old Purdue University grad who went through the intensive course, says, "The first time I went out on my own, the feeling was unbelievable. Within two weeks, I won my first account." The company, which is expanding the program this year, says the new hires generate more revenue and more shipments per sale than do other salespeople. Executives credit Y's with being hungrier and more easily moldable than other sales reps.

I loved . . .

–Gaining customer buy-in on my competence.

–Identifying a solution, proposing a solution, adopting a solution. It was very satisfying to take it all the way through the process.

–Seeing my product launched . . . I was really involved.

Ask your potential peers whether their ideas are listened to and their work has real impact, and ask for examples. Make sure you will have an opportunity to make a real contribution.

–I'm never doing the same thing for one whole week.

–Every day is different . . . every day a new fresh load of issues.

variety

Will your job provide the opportunity to multitask? To do different things throughout the day? Y's have a strong preference for variety.

the bottom line

There are a lot of things to keep in mind as you evaluate positions. Fortunately, most Y's have help. Parents and professors provide active support for most of you. Don't hesitate to reach out to them. I hope you find exactly the job that works for you.

9. leverage your advantages

This chapter is about confidence—the confidence you should rightly have—and points to keep in mind as you go out into the job market.

The work world may not be quite ready for you, but it needs you. It needs your fresh ideas and your energy. It needs your skills and educated minds. And the plain truth is that it needs your raw numbers.

The workplace is undergoing a change. Over the years ahead, you will experience a shift in power and increasing options for reshaping your relationship with those who seek to employ you. You have an important opportunity to rethink the relationship between individuals and "work."

Your power stems from three big advantages:

✓ **A tightening labor market:** You are entering the economy at a time when most companies are becoming increasingly concerned about attracting and retaining talent. We are transitioning from a buyer's market, in which jobs were generally scarce and employers could be highly selective, to a seller's market. Over the decades ahead, demand for talented workers will outstrip supply. Although there will be short-term ups and downs, in general, Western economies have the potential to create more jobs, particularly for college-educated workers, than your generation can fill. Boomers who delay retirement will pick up some of the slack, but you will have the leverage to request arrangements that work best for you. Because you are a large generation, your preferences and needs matter; the business world can't get along without you.

✓ **The ability to take (some) risks:** You have time and a safety net. Blessed with a long life expectancy, you have a horizon that will allow you to develop multiple careers, make and lose fortunes, head in multiple directions, and start over a number of times. Most of you also have uncommonly strong relationships with your family and confidence that your parents, in particular, will be there for you in a pinch. This unflagging support allows you to approach your career with a greater sense of experimentation than past generations enjoyed.

✓ **A distinct point of view:** Without even trying, what you bring to the party is new. You are the first generation to have been reared in a wired, global world. The way you get things done is different from the ways used by those older than you. You have an intuitive understanding of things that others have had to learn through an intellectual process. As a result, you will certainly bring innovation to the world around you by sharing your ideas of how things might work.

This chapter is about these three wonderful advantages lined up on your side. I hope as you review it you'll marshal thoughts that will carry you with confidence into your meetings with potential employers to seal the deal on a great job.

a tightening labor market

You will benefit from both the raw numbers—the sheer number of people who will be available to work over the next decade in comparison with the number of jobs that are likely to be available—and a mismatch between the educational background of the workforce and the skill sets that are in greatest demand. First, let's consider the numbers.

the numbers

You are the biggest generation in history—but not big enough.
Although your generation is huge, larger than the Boomers in the United States, it's not big enough to replace all the Boomers who are eligible for retirement and still provide the upside capacity for the economy's growth. The number of jobs available has increased substantially over the forty years since the Boomers entered the job market. In the United States, if all the Boomers retire, your generation will barely be able fill

the open spots. In many other parts of the world, your numbers are actually fewer than the group retiring. Going forward, the gap between the demand for skilled workers and the available labor pool is expected to widen in industry after industry, region after region, throughout the United States and around much of the world.

This is a happy situation for you. The work world you are entering is reminiscent of the situation your Boomer parents encountered, as described by *Fortune* magazine in 1969: "Because the demand for their services so greatly exceeds the supply, young graduates are in a strong position to dictate terms to their prospective employers. Young employees are demanding that they be given productive tasks to do from the first day of work, and that the people they work for notice and react to their performance."[1] And it's a sharp contrast to the plight of the Gen X'ers when they entered the work world: "[T]hese pioneers of the baby-bust generation are finding life on the career frontier harsher than ever . . . They're snarled in a demographic traffic jam . . . stuck behind all those surplus graduates of the past decade."[2]

Over the next several decades, the U.S. workforce will grow by less than half a percent per year. U.S. businesses are accustomed to much faster growth: over the past several decades, the workforce grew two to three times as fast as it will going forward (see figure 9-1). From 1980 to 2000, the number of people in the twenty-five to fifty-four age group—historically the prime source of the nation's workforce—increased by 35 million in the United States. From 2000 to 2020, it will likely grow by only *3* million. If retirement continues at historic rates,

FIGURE 9-1

Changes in the U.S. working-age population

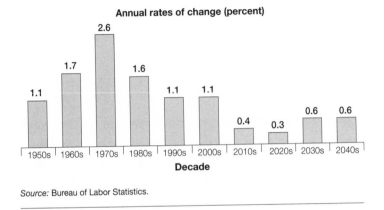

Annual rates of change (percent)

Source: Bureau of Labor Statistics.

the current decade alone will see an exodus of 24 million work-ers, representing 18 percent of the experienced workforce.[3]

The same types of shortages are occurring in Europe, and in many of those countries they are even more severe. Europe's pop-ulation will actually decline over future decades. In the twenty-five countries that make up the European Union, the workforce (here, individuals between fifteen and sixty-four) will shrink by more than 15 percent, or *52 million* workers, between 2004 and 2050: from 307 million to 255 million.[4]

These projections are based on two assumptions. One of these is not really an assumption, but a fact, and the second one is admittedly a lousy assumption. The fact is that we are having many fewer children: birthrates in the United States have fallen from the three-plus children per family born in the

1950s and 1960s to only two children for every two adults; in other words, we are only replacing ourselves. Many countries around the world have birthrates that are much lower than replacement levels. In Italy, for example, the average birthrate is only 1.2 children for every two adults. At this rate, it's possible that the Italian culture will virtually disappear within this century. There won't be enough Italians in Italy for it to feel "Italian."

The second assumption is that your parents, and others of their generation, will stop working—retire—at the same ages adults have done so during the past decade. In many countries, the retirement age for men has been falling; in the United States, it has decreased from age sixty-seven in 1960 to about sixty-four in 2004. In France, the comparable decline is from sixty-five to fifty-nine.

But assuming that retirement ages will remain this low (or that the downward trend will continue) is not a good assumption. We're already seeing evidence that people want to work later in life; many probably are doing so now and are not being captured in the official statistics. During the next decade, I expect to see official retirement ages *increase*, as increasing numbers of individuals choose to remain in the workforce.

Some experts have projected a shortage of 8 million workers in the United States by 2014.[5] However, in that same year, there will be approximately 14 million largely capable adults between the ages of sixty-five and seventy-four, historically a group that would not be actively involved in corporate work or counted in the statistics. If even half of these individuals continue working, their participation would virtually eliminate any potential gap. Because many of these people have skills and experience that most companies will desperately need, they would not only fill slots but also fill specific capability gaps. I suspect that many of them will choose to work, at least part-time, alleviating some of the shortage in key skills.

But don't worry—there will still be lots of jobs for you. Most of the Boomers don't want to work as long or as hard as they have during the past couple of decades. Almost all of them want to cut back—to work part-time or on some other flexible basis. And of course, some don't want to work at all, or at least not in the commercial world; they may be headed for charitable endeavors or other pursuits. The bottom line is that even if you make some aggressive assumptions about the number of older Americans who remain active in the business world, there will still be plenty of gaps in the workforce—and plenty of room for you.

When people predict that there won't be enough jobs in the United States going forward, they often point to three other concerns: global sourcing, immigration, and productivity increases. But these factors are not likely to diminish your prospects significantly. Although some jobs are moving out of high-wage countries into lower-wage emerging economies, that trend has limits. Wages are rising quickly in these recipient economies, and competition for qualified candidates is fierce. Many companies are reevaluating the trade-offs and electing to keep a higher proportion of their jobs in developed economies. Outsourcing is highly disruptive because it has a disproportionate impact in one local community, but overall, even if every job that can possibly be done in a distant location is outsourced, labor shortages will still exist in developed countries. You may need to relocate, but there will be jobs available in some region of the country.

Immigration is of concern to those who feel that domestic jobs are being lost to low-cost immigrant labor. In fact, immigration adds only modestly to the size of the workforce in the United States and serves to augment the reduced flow of native-born workers into the workforce caused by slowing birthrates. Immigration is not expected to be sufficient—even over the medium term—to eliminate the looming talent gap, certainly not in jobs that require college educations.

And neither are increases in productivity—the amount of output produced per hour of work. Even with productivity increases that are already higher than the historical average, the growing talent gap is still evident. Companies cannot realistically expect still greater productivity to solve the workforce crisis.

The bottom line: you are entering the workforce at a time when, in all likelihood, the number of jobs will be plentiful.

education

For those of you with a college education, or headed in that direction, the demand for your presence in the workforce will be greater than the demand that exists for bodies alone.

Jobs in the developed world are shifting to knowledge-based work. Knowledge work makes up an estimated 40 percent of U.S. jobs and accounts for 70 percent of job growth since 1998.[6] Growth in demand for individuals with college-level skills is outstripping supply.

As I discussed in chapter 1, more of you will graduate from college than any generation before you. But the increase won't be enough to keep pace with the shifting economy.[7] The gap between the output of our educational system and job requirements is already significant in many sectors, and growing wider. The mismatch between the shape of the workforce by educational degree and the shape of the available jobs is shown in figure 9-2.

From an employer's perspective, the looming shortage of college-educated workers in the United States is even more severe than the raw numbers suggest, because a significant proportion of the educational capacity in the United States is devoted to students from overseas. For example, about 40 percent of the Massachusetts Institute of Technology's graduate students come from abroad. As recently as a decade ago, most

FIGURE 9-2

The disconnect between talent supply and demand

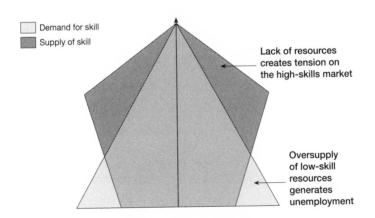

Demand for skill
Supply of skill

Lack of resources creates tension on the high-skills market

Oversupply of low-skill resources generates unemployment

Source: "Confronting the Talent Crunch: 2007," whitepaper, Manpower Inc., 2007.

of these graduates stayed and became critically important members of the U.S. workforce. Today, however, many are returning to their home countries after they've completed their education.[8]

And, because significantly more women than men have college and advanced degrees, to the extent women opt out of the workforce at higher rates, corporations lose a disproportionate percentage of the college-educated workforce.

The bottom line: the mismatch between your generation's education patterns and the skills required in key sectors of the economy will create strong demand for talent.

the ability to take (some) risk

You have time and, in most cases, a safety net. These advantages will allow you to approach your career choices with a greater sense of experimentation than in generations past. You can try work options, and if you fail—or if your first endeavor turns out to be something that doesn't work for you—you can regroup and try again.

Your expanded time horizon stems from your remarkable longevity.

How would you set your work priorities if I said you had only twenty or thirty years to do everything you wanted to do? I think you'd probably be cautious, focused on doing "it" right the first time. But in your case, the choice you make today does not need to be "it." Life expectancies have shot up over the past century, almost doubling in most countries around the world. Most of you will probably have something like *sixty to eighty years* of healthy, active adult life.

So don't freeze up. Don't worry that you're making a decision today that you will have to stick with for the rest of your
life. Be willing to try one career, confident that if it doesn't turn
out to be what you'd like, you'll have plenty of opportunity to
start up another path. You have time.

Most of you have something else as well: a certain level of
emotional and, in some cases, financial support. Your strong,
positive relationships with your parents provide a safety net and,
for many of you, a significant, tangible benefit. According to the
2000 U.S. Census, 4 million people between the ages of twenty-
five and thirty-four live with their parents. Even when you leave
home, many of you are likely to remain in close physical proximity to your parents and extended family over the course of your
life, drawn together by shared interests, affection, and respect.

You have the gift of approaching your careers somewhat op-
portunistically. You have long life expectancies, backup, and
support. Y's are in no hurry. Most of you don't even wear a
watch.

a distinct point of view

You may not realize this, but most of the older adults in the
world don't think or act the way you do.

A number of years ago, a ski instructor told me that he could
always tell whether a person learned to ski as an adult or as a
child. In his experience, even though you could become a very
good skier as an adult, you would never ski in exactly the same
way that you would had you learned as a child.

There's a parallel in this story to the use of technology. Older
adults have learned to use the available technology, but many

of them use it in ways that are fundamentally different from the way you do. You woke up in a world that was fully wired. Many of you booted up before you climbed onto bikes. Technology for you is ubiquitous and an essential part of how you operate day-to-day. You are plugged-in citizens of a worldwide community. You absorbed intuitively things that others have learned intellectually. As I've mentioned before, when it comes to technology, you are unconsciously competent.

Much of my career has been spent studying innovation and helping organizations become more creative. Here's the bottom line: the heart of innovation is to combine two previously unrelated ideas. Sometimes this combination—the innovation— happens within one individual's mind; he or she has an "aha" moment as a connection is made. But more often than not, it comes from two or more people getting together, each with a unique perspective or expertise, and is based on sharing ideas, coming up with something that none of them would have thought of on his or her own.

Inevitably, you will bring innovation to the workplace because the ideas you have about how things might work will almost certainly be new and largely unrelated to the way things have been done for the past fifty years. As a result, you will catalyze innovation in the world around you, simply by sharing your ideas on how things might work.

Your real gift is not so much that you know *how* to use the technology; it's that the *way* you use the technology causes you to think and act differently. Let's look at a few of your unique perspectives and their implications for the contributions you can make to business.

you find new uses for technology
that's "good enough"

One of the legendary stories that circulated around Arthur D. Little, the renowned think tank consulting company where I began my professional career, was about a new technology that had been brought to the firm for evaluation by its inventor. This new technology allowed people to make low-quality duplicates of documents. The very smart consultants concluded that there was little market potential for the product. Who wanted crummy copies of documents?

This was in the early 1940s (long before my time). The technology was xerography, and the rest, as they say, is history. The company that eventually adopted the invention (and changed its company name to Xerox) marketed the machine successfully, and, in doing so, it fundamentally changed many of the ways things got done. People didn't use the machines only to make a few copies of valuable documents; xerography allowed them to make millions of copies of millions of things, using paper in entirely new ways for sharing information and ideas.

You are already playing this game. You are rapidly adopting and popularizing uses for technology that begin by *lowering* the quality standards, but in ways that fundamentally change the patterns of use.

Text messaging and camera phones are two prime examples. Both applications traded off poorer quality for a different level of functionality; e-mail allows longer messages than texting, and, without question, a 35 mm camera takes pictures superior to those snapped by the early camera phones. But whenever you limit a new technology in this way, asking whether it will be of comparable quality to the existing approach, you miss another critical question: will it allow us to do things that we've never done before?

You have led the way in finding dramatic new uses for technology that is barely "good enough." Texting was first observed among Finnish teenagers—not invented by their parents at Nokia, but developed through the creativity of youth. And you have pioneered the lightning-fast spread of camera phones into hundreds of new ways to use "instant" pictures.

This willingness to push the boundaries of "good enough" into new applications will be a great asset in business innovation.

you are comfortable living asynchronously

You are highly accomplished at *time-shifting*—doing things when it is most convenient for you rather than when the world might otherwise think it's scheduled to occur. Watch TV? Not when the programs are broadcast, but on TiVo replay. Share news with friends? Not with a phone call, but with a post on Facebook to be read at your friends' convenience. Listen to music? On your iPod, shifting away from the broadcast schedules imposed by radio.

You live what I call *asynchronous lives*. Technology helps you do many activities anytime, anywhere.

In our discussions, Y's who have been in the workplace for only a year or two say that one of their biggest surprises has been how inefficient most corporate processes seem. They are astonished by the amount of time corporations invest in trying to synchronize participation in a teleconference or, even worse, pulling everyone physically together for a face-to-face meeting, compared with the speed and ease with which they interact with their friends.

With your generation, time-shifting will come to the workplace. You will teach your older coworkers the efficiency of working asynchronously. Your amazing comfort with the use of technology to make your life more efficient will have an important business impact.

You may even help free the workplace of corporate life's rigid schedules. As one young worker demanded of executives in our recent research, "What *is it* with you people and 8:30 a.m.?"

you coordinate rather than plan

Think about how you manage your social activities. I suspect that you rarely, if ever, suggest to your friends on Wednesday that you all meet at a particular place and time on Saturday. Instead, you wait until Saturday and then coordinate, largely through text messaging. You share information about your current location, where you are headed, and when you will arrive—homing in on your friends like ships using radar.

Again, this may seem obvious to you, but it really is quite different from the way older generations operate. They schedule; you don't. You use technology for nearly constant coordination.

You will bring this practice to the workplace. Your work in the future will, in all likelihood, involve much more coordinating and far less planning than is common in most organizations today. For a number of activities, that approach will prove more efficient.

you use multiple technologies simultaneously

Not only do you use technology comfortably, you also use multiple technologies simultaneously, each for its best-suited purpose. You multitask, dividing your activities into long-term and short-term units.

You send a document to your boss for comments by e-mail, and, while waiting for a response, you IM colleagues with questions to which you need immediate answers, post the most recent draft of your analysis on the company's shared Web page, update your Facebook page so that your friends can see your latest weekend photos, and leave a voicemail message for your friend's parents, thanking them for their recent hospitality. Our focus groups revealed that mixing and matching the technologies is an efficient way of managing a number of tasks.

Most of you use two or more communication technologies every day and, in general, are used to being pretty fast; the "instant" in IM is indicative of your operating style. If you haven't encountered it already, I suspect you may be surprised and frustrated with the pace at which many businesses run—the slow tempo of decision making, the number of people who need to sign off, and the time required to have your questions answered. In the workplace, you would clearly prefer the same speed and flexibility you enjoy in your personal lives.

Anecdotal evidence hints that you may be faster at some, if not many, tasks than your older colleagues. One executive told me that she had hired her sixteen-year-old daughter to substitute for members of her department who were on holiday throughout the summer. According to this (OK, very proud) mother, the sixteen-year-old managed to complete each vaca-tioning staff member's normal forty-hour-per-week workload in about three-quarters of that time. By Thursday of each week, the young substitute was looking around for something else to do!

You will bring to the workplace the need for speed and the habit of using the most effective technology for each task.

you solve problems and perform tasks collaboratively

Because the technologies you use allow you to share informa-tion easily, you are inclined to solve problems by tapping com-munal wisdom. However, the level of collaboration that you typically employ is likely to fall outside the norm in most corpo-rations. Many Y's are find that their preferred approach runs counter to corporations' individually oriented compensation and performance management systems and, in some instances, pro-tocols regarding the protection of intellectual property. Reach-ing out freely to tap those whose credibility you vet through your network as sources of the information you need—friends, former colleagues, even contacts at other corporations—seems logical to you, but not necessarily to older colleagues.

But collaboration—sharing and synthesizing knowledge—is becoming increasingly important to organizations. Your skill in this area will come to be appreciated.

you understand how to build and use digital networks

Have you heard the old saying, "He who has money, makes money"? Today, that's not nearly as true as it used to be. The importance of financial capital is giving way to social capital. The unit of economic value is becoming the number of relationships you have.

Somewhere at the heart of what makes your generation different from all others before you is your unique experience with relationships. Your networks are different from those of older generations. They tend to be larger, denser, and composed of a greater proportion of what network theorists call *weak ties* (people we know, but not very well), which is the type considered key for innovation.

At one point, it was believed that the maximum number of relationships one human could form was 150, a figure directly related to the size of the brain's neocortex.[9] Thanks largely to the Internet, many of you have hundreds or even thousands of "friends."[10]

Your weak ties are the relationships that offer new, perhaps conflicting perspectives, provocative insights, and critical connections. In fact, most of us have only three to six *strong ties*— stable relationships that extend over many years and are based on trust, reciprocity, and support (men average three, and women, six).

You use your networks differently than do your elders. You actively engage with your networks in ways that build your reputation. In the words of researcher Michael Carter, "Gen Y's are all about building a reputation, whether online or in the real world . . . The community shapes your reputation."[11] Whether through Amazon.com's collaborative filtering referral system or World of Warcraft's guilds, being rated highly by your peers and being valued as a critic yourself are very important.

Networks change the way things get done. Recent studies of informal networks reveal how much information flows through them and how little goes through official hierarchical structures.[12] Because they do not take into account formal titles or positions, they open the door for smart people at all levels to contribute. In networks, new knowledge is not sent "up" any formal chain of command to be vetted and approved; rather, it is posted broadly or sent, via the network, to people who are believed to be most interested or most in the need to know. You can tap into your network to get jobs, to exchange knowledge or experiences, and to get ideas on how to find relevant information or solve problems.

The peer-to-peer experience will increasingly play out in the corporate world. Your skill in networking will be another important workplace asset.

you are comfortable working anywhere, and alone

The increasing prevalence of non-office-based working arrangements means that many of you will also work physically alone (although you may be "alone" in a Starbucks, surrounded by dozens of other telecommuters).

You may even find yourself working in a virtual world at some point in the future. In the online three-dimensional world Second Life, more than 7 million people (as of this writing) from around the globe already "live," meet, form relationships, exchange information, and conduct business. Individuals participate not as themselves, but through their avatars (computer representations of who they would like to be). Many "first life" commercial companies have already established a presence in Second Life and need employees—real people willing to staff the virtual stores.

In your comfort with working alone, you are shifting the definition of work. Boomers often say they *go to* work. Y's more typically refer to work as something they *do*, accepting that work can happen whenever and wherever they choose.

you redraw the line between institutional and personal technology

You comfortably assume a degree of personal ownership and control over "your" technology. In your world, technology is not the domain of the specialist, and it is as much an extension of you as a handbag or briefcase may be of your parents. Computers are your address books, calendars, photo albums, music machines, and notepads all rolled into one. You store your life in a computer—not only information but also your contacts, photos, and favorite music.

Most Y's entering the workforce already literally own their own technology. Many of you don't want to use the corporate computer, which in many cases is less sophisticated than yours. Y's in our focus groups frequently comment that they have to unlearn how to do something in order to use the company's old systems.

Soon the concept of corporations supplying computers (and cell phones) will be as outdated as the clothing allowances of the 1950s or the company-supplied calculators of the 1970s. All tomorrow's employees will ask is that the company beam them in.

You take ownership in another way as well. You verify before you trust. You have learned early on that appearances can be deceiving. You understand, for example, that photos can be doctored.

This attitude toward the technology will serve you well in tomorrow's workplace.

. . . . .

These three advantages—your numbers, your safety net, and your different point of view—mean that you have a strong wind blowing at your back as you enter the world of work. They give you leverage to shape relationships with employers that will work for you. The time you have and your safety net will allow you to take some risks and experiment more than past generations did. And your distinct point of view will certainly bring innovation to the world around you when you share your ideas on how things might work.

You've got a lot going for you—and a lot to offer to the world of business. Use these strengths to find a career you love.

you got the job—
now what?

Here's an analogy someone shared with me: when you first enter a new organization, your coworkers pull their "cameras" out of their desk drawers and take a picture of you. In essence, they form an impression—of how capable you are, how dependable, the range of your skills. Then, being busy people, they file the photo away.

There is an old saying that you have only one chance to make a first impression. Fortunately, that's not completely true, but it is up to you to create reasons for people to pull those cameras back out of the desk drawer when you're ready for a second look. You need to *plug in*, connect to people, and make a substantive contribution to the essential activities of the organization.

This part of the book is about doing just that.

In chapter 10, I share some perspectives on your future colleagues. The role work will play in your life will probably be quite different from what it was for your parents, and certainly for your grandparents. My goal is not to stereotype people but, I hope, to give you a better sense of why the people you meet in the workplace may approach things in ways that seem a bit odd to you—and what you can do to bridge any gap you may find. I profile the three older generations represented in today's workplace:

✓ Traditionalists

✓ Boomers

✓ Generation X

Understanding the evolution of how each generation views work will, I hope, help you interact with future colleagues more effectively.

In chapters 11 and 12, I offer my perspectives on some of the key skills that you will need at work: hard skills such as writing and finance, and the soft skills that are necessary to relate effectively and continue the good impressions you've undoubtedly made during the interview process. These are chosen to help you make a good first impression and even better impressions over time. They are skills that I believe are critical in the changing workplace.

Today, one-third of new employees begin investigating alternative employment options within six months of being hired.[1] This stems from choosing a place that doesn't fit with your preference and passions—the types of issues I discuss in part II. It's also a result of not integrating effectively once you're there. That's the point of part III—plugging in.

10. make a multigenerational workforce work for you

Why do *they* do what they do?

Today, you are sharing the workplace with individuals from three other generations, each shaped by markedly different teen experiences and now approaching work with diverse assumptions about how the world works and what they want from life:

✓ **The Traditionalists:** Born between 1928 and 1945

✓ **The Boomers:** Born between 1946 and 1964

✓ **Generation X:** Born between 1965 and 1979

The backgrounds that shaped these generations have significant implications for the role that work plays in their lives, what they expect to receive from the work experience, and how they are likely to judge your actions and performance, fairly or not. Rather than be frustrated by these differences, it's better to understand them and use that understanding to help plug in with each individual effectively. Working with people of all ages is critical to your success in a multigenerational workplace. Understanding why colleagues from other generations might behave the way they do will give you an advantage as you work with them—whether they be your bosses, colleagues, clients, partners, or customers.

As you read this chapter, you'll be imagining what it would have been like to be a teenager during each generation's formative moment in time. Each time, ask yourself, "What assumptions would I logically have formed about how the world works if this were the world I saw? Whom would I respect and trust? What would I expect to do with my life? How would I measure its success?"

I hope that doing this will give you some useful insights into what "they" might be thinking, will make the work world seem a little more understandable, and will help you steer clear of some of the unfortunate misunderstandings that seem common in the workplace. By understanding the perspectives of other generations, you will be better able to position your ideas and requests in ways that are likely to have positive results.

traditionalists

It's particularly important to understand people who belong to this generation because even though their presence in the workplace is decreasing, many of their assumptions are deeply embedded in the fabric of organizations. The very corporations where you are or might soon be working are the result of the teen experiences of the generation that may have included your grandparents.

Also known as the WWII (or Silent) generation, Traditionalists were children during World War II, but, importantly, many were teens in the hustle-bustle postwar years.

---

traditionalists

BORN: **1928 to 1945**

TEEN YEARS: **1942 to 1963**

IN 2008: **63+ years old**

Key world events during the Traditionalists' teenage years included the resolution of World War II and, later, the Cuban missile crisis—triumphs for government and those in authority. Russia achieved the first manned space flight, and Pan Am, an airline that went out of business before the oldest of you turned twelve, introduced the first round-the-world commercial air flight. The United Kingdom and France become nuclear powers.

In the booming postwar economies of Europe and the United States, opportunity appeared on every street corner. Suburbs popped up, and the dream of home ownership was suddenly within reach. Factories that had made war machines began cranking out washing machines at an astounding rate. Television purchases skyrocketed; by the end of the decade more than 80 percent of all U.S. households owned these new marvels of technology. Family dinner table conversations probably included comments about the amazing new conveniences just acquired by the family down the street, as "keeping up with the Joneses" became a national pastime.

Now, assume that you are a teenager looking at the world for the first time at this moment. What assumptions would you form about how the world works? Whom would you respect and trust? What would you expect to do with your life? How would you measure its success?

As I've said, any theory of this sort involves a bit of generalization, stretching as it does to capture the common characteristics of people in many different circumstances. But for most who grew up in this economy of grand promise and endless optimism, this was a world that probably appeared to be heading in the right direction. Authority figures seemed to have things well in hand. Corporate leaders and government officials warranted respect. Global issues were being resolved in reasonably satisfactory ways, and technology promised an alluring future. Financial success became a logical life goal. It would be natural for any teen living at this time to leap enthusiastically into the work world if possible, to become part of the existing establishment and attain the financial rewards that it promised—to get a piece of the pie.

There were important exceptions to this sense of unlimited optimism, based primarily on people's perceived access to this promising world. For minority teens, particularly African Americans, the world held the same allure but not the same sense of attainability. The path to personal success was then much less clear. But this was a world where a logical desire would be to *want to join* it; the train was moving out of the station and headed in the right direction. The goal was to get on board and achieve for yourself the prosperity promised along the way.

By and large, the business organizations built by Traditionalists reflect these values. This generation constructed many of today's most successful corporations based on practices that made sense at the time: hierarchical roles, chains of command, structured career paths, banded salary levels, and well-planned, multiyear strategies. Traditionalists tend to be respectful of authority and comfortable in hierarchical organizations; they see value in stability and assume that fairness is provided by consistently applied rules (the same for everyone).

It's not hard to see why Traditionalists might be reluctant to make major changes in the way things have "always" been done. To you, they are likely to appear rule bound. And although things may be slowly changing, you'll find that the current structures, management practices, and policies shaped by these values are still in place in most corporations.

Traditionalists tend to be strongly influenced by financial reward and the security it can bring. Of course, most people—in any generation—appreciate and, to one degree or another, are motivated by monetary rewards. For Traditionalists, however, money has an almost symbolic role. It serves as a metric for achievement of their important teenage goal. By achieving financial rewards, they affirm to themselves and others that they have indeed gotten their piece of the pie.

This assumption—that money is everyone's dominant motivator and reward—is one of the most common sources of misunderstanding between corporations and Generation Y employees. You'll run into many senior managers, some a bit younger than the Traditionalists, who have a hard time understanding the trade-offs you are making and the role that money plays in your decisions.

Over the next several decades, Traditionalists will continue to participate in the workplace. Although almost all of them are (or soon will be) of conventional retirement age, many are already choosing to continue working in a variety of ways. Going forward, as you work with them, keep in mind the importance they place on financial recognition, security, and hierarchy. Individuals in this generation are not likely to be effective and engaged participants in the workforce unless these assumptions about how things are supposed to work are acknowledged and, to the extent possible, accommodated.

To them, you look, above all . . . young. Most Traditionalists that I've interviewed are confident that you're going to "grow out" of some of your more distinctive Gen Y views—for example, that you'll come to place the same value on money and security that they do when you get a bit older. Or that your sense of immediacy will diminish and you will assume a longer-term, deferral-based perspective on life.

Table 10-1 shows examples of some of the situations that you may encounter in which a Traditionalist is likely to see things differently than you do.

Success with most individuals in the Traditionalist generation requires, at a basic level, respect for them and the companies they've built. You need to acknowledge the legitimacy of their rules and adopt an attitude that comes across as, "I can see why that was a great way to do it, but now that [something

TABLE 10-1

Different perspectives: Traditionalists and Generation Y

Situation	Traditionalists see . . .	Y's think . . .
Your parents are actively and visibly involved in the recruiting and hiring process, mailing your résumé, confirming your interview times, driving you to interviews.	A candidate who is overly dependent on others and perhaps unable to think for himself.	This is a normal and logical way to involve people who are ready and willing to help out with some of the mundane tasks and likely to have relevant expertise.
You get a job offer that has attractive financial benefits, but another firm's offer includes paid time off to do community service.	A no-brainer—isn't money the reason people work? Of course you'll choose the offer with the greatest compensation.	I need enough money, but not the most I can possibly make. I'm willing to trade off money for other things I care deeply about.
Your initial month at the company is spent in a training program, providing you with step-by-step knowledge of how to do the assigned task.	A sensible relationship between training and doing—pay your dues and learn our way first.	BO-ring! I'd much rather figure it out myself as I go.
You have an idea that could represent a real opportunity to improve, and you send a suggestion to the CEO.	A shocking breach of proper hierarchical behavior. *Everyone* knows ideas should go up the chain of command.	Why waste time? Send any idea or question to the person who is most likely to benefit from it.
You are invited to dinner at your boss's home. He clearly assumes that your new spouse will be there as well, but you show up alone.	Is this Y's spouse supportive of his or her career? Spouses should publicly demonstrate their enthusiasm and commitment to your work.	Are you kidding?! My spouse is an independent person with his or her own priorities. The days of "two for the price of one" are long gone.
The company has no policy that allows sabbaticals or even unpaid leave. You have a once-in-a-lifetime opportunity to do something that requires two months off. You request the time.	This situation could set a dangerous precedent. Rules are rules; you need to conform to ours.	How ridiculous! Rules should be adapted to make sense for the situation at hand.

(continued)

TABLE 10-1 *(continued)*

Different perspectives: Traditionalists and Generation Y

Situation	Traditionalists see . . .	Y's think . . .
You routinely finish your work by 4 p.m. and offer to help others. When no one takes you up on the offer, you head home early.	A slacker—we're paying for eight hours a day; you need to stay here. Work is a place you go to for a specified period of time.	Work is something you do—anytime, anywhere. If there's no "work" to be done, why stay?
You find the work being done in another department intriguing and ask for a lateral transfer. You are told that you were up for a promotion in your old department but will have to "start over" at the bottom in the new group.	A puzzling move. Wouldn't the opportunity to gain more positional authority (and money) trump an intriguing job?	So?
You are feeling restless and openly discuss with your colleagues your interest in moving to another firm.	Unacceptable behavior. Loyalty to the firm is essential, and this is a clear sign of disloyalty. Moreover, you could incite disloyalty among colleagues by discussing your thoughts openly.	Who better to bounce these concerns off than colleagues, who may be feeling them as well?
You announce you're leaving the company.	A dumb move. If you'd stayed another thirty years, you would have had the security of being able to retire with a solid pension.	On to new adventures!

has changed] let's consider whether there might be a better way." In the next chapters, I talk more about some of the specific approaches that I've found most effective in initiating changes successfully.

In addition, it is important that you recognize that a Traditionalist's offer of additional monetary compensation is a big deal, and a great compliment.

boomers

For many of you, Boomers are your parents. Their teen years—the time when they in all likelihood took their first good look at the world and formed their most vivid and lasting impressions of how things work—were during the 1960s and 1970s. This was a time when the world was changing radically, yielding a generation with dramatically different perspectives from their Traditionalist parents' about the type of relationships they would form with corporations, peers, and family; about the importance and definition of financial success; and about the ultimate objectives for their lives.

---

boomers

BORN: **1946 to 1964**

TEEN YEARS: **1960 to 1982**

IN 2008: **44 to 62 years old**

Boomers' teen years were filled with causes and revolution. The 1960s and 1970s were decades of general unrest and discontent in many parts of the world. In the United States, teenage Boomers saw the assassinations of idealistic leaders—John F. Kennedy, Robert F. Kennedy, Malcolm X, and Martin Luther King Jr. They experienced the Vietnam War, widespread protests, the civil rights movement, and, toward the end of their teen years, the Watergate scandal and the resignation of President Richard Nixon.

The sense of unrest was pervasive in many parts of the world. Nearly three hundred thousand so-called boat people fled Vietnam; the Cultural Revolution was under way in the People's Republic of China; there was rioting in France, Germany, and Italy, and a revolution in the former Czechoslovakia.

Not surprisingly, growing up amid these events caused many Boomers to conclude that the world was not working very well and needed to change. Many, regardless of political persuasion, concluded that the world did not appear to be headed in the right direction.

Even worse to many Boomers, the adults in charge didn't appear to be making the right decisions or setting the right course, or necessarily even telling the truth. Many Boomers developed skeptical, even cynical, attitudes toward authority. Their world was one in which authority figures were suspect. Many concluded that they needed to get personally involved. Their logical desire, based on their teen experiences, was not, like the Traditionalists', to *join* a world that was by and large headed in the right direction, but instead was to *change* a world that clearly had gone off course.

This fundamental difference in life view has played out in several important ways. As I noted in chapter 1, perhaps most important for you is that many Boomers did not see eye-to-eye with their parents. Most Boomers couldn't wait to escape from their parents' control, moving to distant locations and creating independent lives as soon as possible. This, in turn, affects the judgments they form about you; they are puzzled about your closeness to your families and wonder whether it means you are in some way less competent or ambitious than they were at your age. As I discuss later in this chapter, I don't think that's an accurate view, but it is a reality of the world you're entering.

As a result of their common teenage experiences, many Boomers tend to harbor a significant seed of antiauthoritarian sentiment. Although they may be in leadership positions, many remain skeptical of positional leaders. No matter how buttoned-up a Boomer colleague may seem to be, there's usually an instinct to question and, to some extent, resist hierarchy. To this extent, they may be natural allies for you.

Boomers also retain a strong sense of idealism. Although many have dedicated the past thirty years of their lives to building careers, paying mortgages, and rearing children, most Boomers still have a deep desire to make a difference in the world. Again, these values echo many of yours and position Boomers as logical partners to further some of your life goals.

But—and here's the big difference between your generation and theirs—Boomers tend to be highly competitive and extremely driven. When they looked around during their teenage years, the other major thing they saw was . . . lots of other Boomer teenagers. They grew up in a crowded world—with the largest group of peers yet—at a time when much of their immediate world was "too small" for the size of the generation. Many Boomers went to high school in Quonset huts or other temporary buildings, because the existing schools were too small to accommodate this new bulge of students. They have competed for virtually everything all their lives—a seat in nursery school, a place on the high school sports team, college admissions, and every step of their career progression. Boomers, as a generation, have learned to value individual achievement and individual recognition. Competition runs deep through all their assumptions about how the world works. Winning, for Boomers, is a *very* big deal.

This competitive streak caused most Boomers to jump into the workforce with passion and commitment. As a generation, they have been hardworking and fantastically productive. They still work longer hours than any other generation. They like merit-based pay systems and use both money and position to measure the degree to which they are winning. They have played life's games with abandon, in some cases without questioning the rules, and have lived life—at least until now—under the axiom, "Whoever dies with the most toys wins." Only recently have they begun to pause to inquire about the true value of the prize.

Notice the subtle but important difference in the role of money for the two generations discussed so far. Traditionalists see money as a symbol that they have successfully joined the business "club" and are reaping the benefits of membership. For Boomers, money tends to be a symbol of competitive success—of winning. Although the significance is slightly different, money works as the primary reward and motivation for both generations and causes both generations to misinterpret the attitude of Y's toward the supremacy of financial rewards.

The Boomers' competitive streak plays out in another way that is important for you to understand: if your parents are Boomers, they are likely to sweep you up into their natural competitive moves. This means that they often may seem more eager for you to succeed (by their standards) than you are yourself. Partnering effectively with your parents—recognizing and appreciating their sincere interest in your success and happiness without getting overtaken by some of their more competitive tendencies—requires attention. In chapter 12, I offer some suggestions on where to draw the line and how to enlist their help in positive ways.

Boomers who are *not* your parents are often ambivalent in their initial view toward Y's. On one hand, many of them have children your age and are rooting for your success. And, willing to be challenged, antiauthoritarian, and idealistic themselves, they admire your rebel spirits.

On the other hand, Boomers played by the rules as they competed their way up the corporate ladders; they may not have liked them much, but they fell in line and played the game. And, to the extent that they were willing to conform to the existing system, some resent your unwillingness to do so. They find you remarkably impatient and comment repeatedly on your reluctance to pay your dues. They are the most likely to judge that whatever you're doing is not being done the way they would have done it when they were your age.

Again, the differences between their outlook and yours can create misunderstandings. Table 10-2 shows examples of some of the situations that you may encounter in which a Boomer is likely to see things differently than you do.

At the core of working successfully with Boomers is finding your common ground. Some common ground will come in the form of your desire to learn and Boomers' enjoyment of teaching and helping you succeed. Boomers, in general, will be wonderful mentors. Seek them out, and enjoy the advice that they'll likely be happy to share.

TABLE 10-2

Different perspectives: Boomers and Generation Y

Situation	Boomers see . . .	Y's think . . .
You have two job offers in hand—one with a prestigious firm on Wall Street, and the second with a small company with flexible hours and no dress code.	A no-brainer. Of course the prestigious job is better. It will demonstrate to others that you've won this round.	If I do take the Wall Street job, it will probably be for a short time, just to get money to pay off my loans. The work style of the other firm is closer to what I prefer.
The company has organized a detailed recruiting process, with an opportunity to meet many executives, who spoke glowingly of the work experience. The ex-employee Web site, however, is very negative.	Job well done—an effective process well implemented . . . What do you mean you're not accepting the job?	I'll always exercise all my sources to get the inside story. With the Internet, you can find out how almost anyone feels about anything.
You see a job opening that looks really interesting. You don't have any of the qualifications listed on the job description, but you're confident you could handle the work. You apply.	A joke! Don't you understand that formal qualifications and degrees are critical evidence of your worth and ability?	My parents always told me I can do anything I set my mind to. I believe that—and have set my mind to do this.
Your résumé lists the six jobs you've held in the four years since leaving college.	Someone who can't make up his mind or settle down—probably a flake. In my day, everyone knew that you couldn't change jobs more often than once every two years.	This is great evidence that I'm willing to take risks and seek out new opportunities.
You move back home to live with your parents for a few months.	Someone who can't take care of herself and is overly dependent on parental support.	It's a sensible way to save money.

(continued)

TABLE 10-2 *(continued)*

Different perspectives: Boomers and Generation Y

Situation	Boomers see . . .	Y's think . . .
You are asked to take on a new role—a position that has not previously existed at the company—tackling an important, urgent, but ambiguous issue. Your boss asks you to spend the first few weeks preparing a detailed job description for approval higher up.	Clearly the best way to begin is to gain consensus on the rules of the game and the way you'll be judged.	What a waste of time. Just give me the tools, latitude, and day-to-day guidance, and I'll get the job done, improvising as necessary as I go.
Your Boomer boss stops by to tell you that you've been selected to become an office head—in another city. You don't want to relocate, so you decline.	Someone who lacks commitment to her career, loyalty to the company, ambition, and confidence. A slacker.	Clawing my way up the corporate ladder is not a priority—or maybe even something I want at all. The move would mess up a number of other important priorities in my life.
Your boss stays in the office until 8 p.m. each day and sometimes comes in on Saturdays. You leave at 5, confident that your work is complete.	Someone who is not fully dedicated to getting ahead. Face time spent in the office is a key sign of commitment. You need to put in at least sixty hours a week to be taken seriously.	It's too bad it takes those older workers so long to get their work done. I work faster and much more efficiently.
You present a proposal for a new campaign and suggest that your boss poll everyone today for input. You plan to launch in a couple of days.	Slow it down! We need to get a meeting scheduled with all the relevant people (and some who only think they're relevant) so that everyone can provide input. It will take at least three weeks to match everyone's calendar.	Collecting input through a synchronous physical meeting is a quaint—and very inefficient—approach. This could be accomplished in a couple of hours on a social networking site.
You let your Boomer boss know that you're not really finding the task you've been assigned satisfying.	A spoiled nuisance. Of course not every task is inherently interesting. That's not my problem. You should focus on the end game—winning longer term. Head down, nose to the grindstone.	Life is filled with uncertainty. I want to enjoy every day fully. Time to look for another job.

(continued)

TABLE 10-2 (*continued*)

Different perspectives: Boomers and Generation Y

Situation	Boomers see . . .	Y's think . . .
Your boss asks you to attend an important sales conference next week. You're hosting a party for your mom's birthday, so you decline.	An unacceptable response. Do you have any idea how many family events— birthdays, recitals, school pageants—I've sacrificed for the company's benefit and in pursuit of my career?	I remember how it felt when Dad and Mom missed my birthday. I'm not going to do that to my kids. She'll only turn two once.
Your boss appoints you to tackle an exciting new business opportunity. You immediately rally your colleagues and ask them to work with you on it.	Someone who just doesn't get it. This is your opportunity to break out of the pack—and you're involving the rest of the pack in your big move. How can I tell that you've won?	Approaching the task collaboratively will result in a better outcome and will be more fun.
You get your first formal feedback from your boss. It focuses on how you rank against your peers and what you can do to get ahead.	A well-designed process. Comparative evaluative feedback is the most important input a boss can provide.	This is disappointing. Why isn't there more emphasis on acknowledging what I have accomplished?
You're asked to become the program manager for an important initiative. Your boss asks to see your detailed plan for how and when you will communicate with the team. You don't have one.	No schedule! It will be impossible to make progress. You need to get a series of meetings on everyone's calendars —now!	No problem. I'll text the group whenever we need to coordinate our moves.
You get invited to a corporate strategy session. The conversation focuses on evaluating which businesses are stronger and deserve additional investment.	A solid, well-accepted process.	I wonder if there might be a better way? Maybe we should be designing experiments to try some new ideas or get some of the weaker businesses repositioned.
A woman is promoted to be the CEO of your company.	A momentous event! All that sacrifice and hard work has paid off. A woman has broken through the glass ceiling!	This is news?

Another form of common ground may come through your shared goals of creating change in the corporate world and beyond. Many of the types of changes you might like in workforce practices are closely aligned with the types of changes Boomers would now like as they look toward adopting flexible schedules at this point in their careers. Team with Boomers to find constructive paths to help organizations adapt to both your needs and theirs.

More broadly, most Boomers have not had, or have not taken, the discretionary time they'd like to make a change in the world. Their passion for life, for change, and for meaning has by no means faded. Many Boomers are finding themselves hit hard with a sense of midlife malaise—an "Is this all there is?" reflection as the end of the first game (the typical thirty-year career) draws near, and a desire to make a positive difference with their remaining time. Finding ways to partner with Boomers to combine your passions for change with theirs presents a powerful opportunity for you to make an even bigger impact on the world around you.

generation x

The generation that immediately precedes you—for some of you, your older siblings; for others, perhaps your parents—has yet again very different characteristics and assumptions. Born between 1965 and 1980, Generation X is much smaller in size than either your generation or the large population of Boomers they followed. They are, in a sense, a sandwich generation—locked between two very large and influential groups of age mates—and not altogether happy about it.

generation x

BORN: 1965 to 1979

TEEN YEARS: 1980 to 1998

IN 2008: 28 to 42 years old

Gen X'ers were teens in the 1980s and 1990s—a very different period from the turbulent 1960s and 1970s. The world stage was much quieter. The cold war had ended, the Berlin Wall had fallen, and, as a result, attention was much less focused on global events. The Vietnam War had ended, and, although important conflicts continued throughout the world, their visibility to most teens in the United States, in particular, was slight.

Much of the focus during this generation's teen years was on the domestic scene—both at a national level and, even more significantly, within the home. Many domestic economies, including those of European countries and the United States, were stagnant. Persistent financial crises flared throughout Latin America.

In contrast to the relative quiet of the world stage, the home front for many teens in this generation was undergoing major change. For the first time, women entered the workforce in significant numbers. This generation's Boomer mothers represented the first real industrial age generation of working women, with 80 percent choosing to work outside the home for reasons other than the extraordinary circumstances of war.

On average, the percentage of women in the workforce during the time Generation X'ers were teens rose from about 35 percent to nearly 60 percent in the United States. The entry of women into the workforce was hastened by the significant increase in divorce rates. Gen X'ers living in the United States saw divorce rates among their parents skyrocket from about 20 percent when they were young to more than 50 percent by the time they were teens.

The women who made this step into the external world of work found that their entry was, in many cases, hard fought and little supported. There was virtually no infrastructure in place—few day care centers, no nanny networks or company-sponsored child care. As a result, the Generation X children became a generation of latchkey kids—home alone many afternoons, often depending on friends for both companionship and support.

Teenage X'ers also witnessed a significant increase in adult unemployment, as reengineering and other corporate restructuring dramatically revamped any concept of lifetime employment. It's unlikely that any person growing up in this generation in the United States would not have known some adult who was laid off from a job that he or she had planned to hold until retirement. It may not have been a parent—perhaps it was a neighbor or a friend's parent—but the sense that adults in their lives were being laid off from corporations that they had depended on for a lifetime commitment is probably the single most widely shared experience of this generation.

The impact of these experiences is not hard to predict. The need for self-reliance and the ability to take care of oneself is deeply embedded in the assumptions many in this generation hold about the world. For support, many rely more on friends than on institutions and even, in some cases, family. Gen X'ers are often reluctant to relocate away from their established "tribe." Most continually question whether the job they have now is still the best opportunity possible and need to be "re-recruited" every day. They are uneasy about putting their fate in the hands of a potentially capricious corporation that could, at any moment, decide to downsize. As a result, many members of Generation X feel a bit out-of-sorts in large corporations. Boomers often judge the X'er to be less committed and less hardworking than Boomers are.

In your eyes, X'ers may lack the technical skills of your own generation. Generation X grew up alongside the Internet—they learned it as it grew—but many don't have the same level of proficiency as most Y's. It was in its infancy when they were in theirs. They are skilled at accessing a wide range of information, but in most cases, they don't have the accompanying behavioral changes discussed in chapters 2 and 9 that many of you do.

Rules have often proven to be a source of conflict between X'ers and the corporations they work for. The mores of the computer games X'ers played as teens extend to many aspects of their lives; to them, rules are interesting, certainly worth con-sidering, but if they don't make sense in the specific situation at hand, X'ers believe in changing them. Holding on to outdated or inapplicable rules for fear of setting a precedent is a nonsen-sical concept to many Gen X'ers. In this, their views probably seem similar to yours; the difference is that they, in most cases, lacked the leverage to push for change. Most X'ers buckled down and followed the rules—and many resent it when it seems you don't have to.

Like you, Generation X as a group has a terrific set of traits that is valuable in our economic society. For example, their independence leads to a strong streak of out-of-the-box thinking and entrepreneurial energy, their tribal behavior enhances any team-based activity, and their lack of a win-at-all-costs mentality raises important questions about the way we all balance work commitments. Many X'ers are avid users of collaborative technology in their personal lives. And, if you form strong relationships, Gen X'ers can be strong allies with Y's in the workplace—in part, because you share a preference for new ways of working.

However, tensions exist. As Bruce Stewart and Brendan Peat of New Paradigm Learning Corporation explain, X'ers are "currently among the most resistant workers within corporations . . . They are deeply conservative in their work styles, and are keen users of e-mail, but are less overtly collaborative in their approach to work. (The formative work experiences seem to have reinforced the importance of 'looking out for yourself.') These people, when in positions of some authority, often become roadblocks to collaboration, forming what we call a 'frozen middle' that is difficult to penetrate. They are often concerned with what their superiors will think, are unwilling to act as a champion, and are uncertain how to act if they 'lose control' of their subordinates."[1]

Understandably, X'ers skills may make this group appear less qualified than Y's when compared with the deep knowledge of Boomer colleagues. In our research, we found Y's who resented Gen X managers and worried that their Boomer allies were being passed over by new X bosses. A sampling from our focus groups: "In a recent reorganization, people with 35 years' experience were 'dropped' behind 3 PhDs . . . It's a joke. They're much more qualified with 25 years of process technology/chemistry experience." "New people don't know what they are talking about. The older people get disgruntled."

And some X'ers find Y's threatening. In our conversations, they worried about your greater technical sophistication and high, fresh energy. Many X'ers feel that they have been stuck in crummy jobs behind the huge bulge of Boomers for a decade or more, counting the days until the Boomers clear out of the workplace. Just as that is beginning, they now face a new wave of competition; you are attractive candidates for the good jobs, just as they're beginning to open up.

Table 10-3 highlights examples of some of the situations that you may encounter in which an X'er is likely to see things differently than you do.

Keep in mind when working with X'ers that one of their strongest values is self-reliance. Motivated by the need to keep as many options open as possible, they share your desire for continuous learning. Consider whether the moves you hope to make can support their goals, and be sensitive to where they are in their lives.

when you're the boss

Over the coming years, you are increasingly likely to have people who are (much) older than you reporting to you. As the overall mix of ages in the workforce shifts so that an increasingly higher percentage are older by definition, bosses will find themselves supervising people who are older than they are. I also expect that many of the Gen Y's who are entering the workforce now will assume leadership roles at earlier ages than

TABLE 10-3

Different perspectives: Generation X and Generation Y

Situation	X'ers see . . .	Y's think . . .
You interview for a job that you're really interested in. You don't hear anything at all from the company for more than a month.	A normal recruiting process, certainly the way it was done when we were job hunting.	A shockingly rude and discouraging reaction on the part of the company. You expect frequent updates on your status. Without that, you look elsewhere.
You are asked to tackle a project that you have no experience doing. You reach out to several Boomer colleagues in other departments for advice on the best way to proceed.	Disrespectful—don't you realize that I'm your supervisor? You should follow protocol. I certainly had to follow the rules.	I'm going after the best sources of information like a heat-seeking missile. Clearly these Boomers know a lot more about the specifics of this problem than my direct boss does.
Your boss assigns you a new project and indicates that you'll be up for review in six months.	A normal performance management process, certainly the way it was done for us.	Are you kidding? You mean we're not going to touch base this afternoon? I'd rather have continual informal feedback.
You confide in your mom how disappointed you are about your most recent performance review. Unbeknownst to you, she calls your boss.	Someone who shows a troubling and highly annoying lack of independence.	Who can control those Boomer parents? All you did was confide in someone you view as a trusted friend and adviser.
You have an idea about how to use a new Web 2.0 collaborative technology in one of your projects. You open a site and post your ideas there.	A good idea, granted, but not one that the company has used before. We need to get everyone up to speed on this new use of technology (especially me—I don't want to be left out of the loop!).	What's to think about? Why wait? This is the obvious way.

(continued)

TABLE 10-3 (*continued*)

Different perspectives: Generation X and Generation Y

Situation	X'ers see . . .	Y's think . . .
You send your ideas and questions to your boss by e-mail or IM as they occur, often six or eight times a day. You rarely get a response.	Someone who is very high maintenance and engages in odd and disruptive behavior that's inconsistent with the way we work.	This is a normal and desirable way to communicate with colleagues. If they have something to say, they'll respond. I wish my boss would shoot me frequent notes.
You add a variety of your favorite programs to the computer your company provided.	A breach of company policy.	Computers are an integral hub for a wide variety of my activities —music, photos, personal contacts. It makes no sense to maintain two systems.
Your boss offers you a role as a first-line supervisor, saying that after you've done it for a year or so you will be qualified for a broad range of next steps.	An attractive next step— one that will increase your self-reliance by providing you with a wide range of possible options for your career.	That job does not look attractive—too much time and paperwork in return for too little additional benefit. And doing it for a year would be much too long. No thanks. I'm enjoying what I'm doing now.
You ask your boss for information about your career path and are given a broad and somewhat vague menu of possible options.	A great response. Doesn't everyone want numerous options and the ability to choose what they prefer?	Pretty lame. The company should do more to outline exciting paths and sit down with me to help customize a successful strategy to meet my needs.
You and a group of your friends decide to resign. You're planning to start your own company.	A great move—loyal to your friends, giving you more self-reliance and control over your destiny.	An adventure I want to try now, while I'm at a point in life where it's easy to take risks. And, if it doesn't work, I can always go home for a while.

we've seen in other generations, in part because of the departure of large numbers of Boomers and the resulting increase in
leadership openings.

Keep in mind that, although it may initially feel awkward for
you, it is also likely to be awkward for the older worker who is
now answering to a younger boss. Although it depends on the
individuals involved, there are several typical complications.
There is likely to be some tension if the older worker is stepping
down from a leadership position or feels in competition with
the younger boss. As I've said, Boomers, in particular, tend to be
competitive and may often have a harder time ceding leadership
than those from other generations do. And, of course, differing
generational perceptions will make it easy to misinterpret each
other's actions.

How can you as the younger boss help make this relationship a successful partnership?

The key, as with any relationship, is to recognize that both
people bring something to the party. The older worker may well
have more experience in the specific industry than the younger
boss, but the younger boss may have some new perspectives
that will improve the way things have "always" been done.
Each individual needs to be open to learning from the other.

It's important for each party to figure out how the other likes
to communicate. Keep in mind that you are very likely to communicate more frequently than your older report is accustomed
to doing. Help older workers see that they should not interpret
frequent messages from you as a sign that you don't trust them,
but rather just as a difference in communication style and habit.
Similarly, you may be used to communicating through different
approaches; your older workers may find that you use much

less face-to-face communication than they are accustomed to. Try to find good ways to meet in the middle.

Avoid coming in with preconceived notions; listen for a while, and ask lots of questions. One of the most common mistakes a young manager can make is thinking that the way it has been done so far has no value. The way things are done may need to change, but it's worth understanding why intelligent people have made the choices they have in the past. The young boss needs to think in terms of "What can I learn here?" as well as "How can I make it better?"

If possible, position your ideas as building on the strengths of the group, rather than repudiating the group's previous approaches. For example, many Y's have experience in collaborative environments; bringing these approaches to the team may offer a new way of working. Integrating technology that makes the work processes faster and easier may be another contribution a young boss can make.

Respect for your leadership is something you'll earn over time, so don't be discouraged. Demonstrate your capabilities, and the respect and trust of your older subordinates will follow. The age difference between a younger boss and older workers need not be a troublesome factor if you each approach the relationship with a spirit of mutual appreciation and shared learning.

. . . . .

Perhaps the most important suggestion of all is simply to remember that the way something looks to you is probably not the way it looks to others. This doesn't mean that members of other generations are wrong. Looking at the situation through their lens will give you a clue about why they do what they do. "Underlying Assumptions: Four Generations" recaps the strikingly different basic worldviews of all four groups.

underlying assumptions: four generations

TRADITIONALISTS: I want to join the world and benefit accordingly.

BOOMERS: I want to help change the world—but I also need to compete to win.

GENERATION X: I can't depend on institutions. I need to keep my options open.

GENERATION Y: I need to live life now—and work toward long-term shared goals.

Remember, it's easy to come to the wrong conclusion about colleagues' motives if you view their actions through your lens and not through theirs. Table 10-4 summarizes a few things to keep in mind.

Bottom line: as you work with people from other generations and other backgrounds, think about their formative years for clues about why they may see things differently than you do. Given their teen experiences, the differences among the four generations at work are striking. Understand them—and work constructively to accomplish common goals.

TABLE 10-4

Y's and the other generations

	How they look to you	How they feel about you
Gen X	• Inexperienced, particularly when compared with Boomer colleagues • Not very sympathetic to your views	• Threatened by your technological sophistication. • Resentful that you are candidates for the "good" jobs just as they're beginning to open up.
Boomers	• Experienced and knowledgeable • Often very supportive, almost parental • Very competitive and obsessively driven	• Frustrated—you seem remarkably unwilling to play by the rules they had to play by. • Ambivalent—they both admire and resent you.
Traditionalists	• Very rigid and rule bound • Very focused on money	• Confident you'll soon outgrow your views—you appear very young. • Confident you'll respond to money.

11. business basics—communication and the language of business

You are the best-educated generation yet, bringing wonderful capabilities into the workforce. However, there are two skills that are essential to success in the work world that you may not have mastered or, in one case, even been exposed to. You must be able to communicate well in writing, using a style that is suitable to business. And you need to understand and comfortably speak a language that is the foundation of any enterprise (including nonprofits): the language of finance.

Generation Y, as a whole, has a bad reputation when it comes to writing, even though I know some of you who do it extraordinarily well. And many of you, particularly those who have eased out of the math and science tracks, may not have been exposed to many key financial concepts or may not feel confident of your ability to speak this language fluently. Both skills will be keys to your success.

It's important. Communication skills are specifically what employers look for in recent graduates. Academic grades are actually at the bottom of the list.[1]

This chapter looks at the first two of the ten tips I've identified specifically for you:

- ✓ **Remember, I'm not a mind reader:** The necessity of clear communication

- ✓ **Reason, reason is my middle name:** The influence of financial logic

don't expect mind readers: communicate openly

I've noticed something interesting. If you ask most people for something openly, clearly, and directly, chances are good that they either will give it to you—even if it's hard for them to do so—or will try hard to propose a reasonable alternative. On the other hand, if you take even the smallest thing without asking, people almost invariably get upset.

One of the most important elements—perhaps *the* most important—of success in the workplace is to make sure people understand your position clearly: what it is and why you believe it's the right way to go. To do this, you must be able to express your thoughts logically, clearly, and persuasively. You must be able to write well.

Bran Ferren, the man who ran Disney's animation studios for many years, predicts that writing will one day go away—disappear as a necessary skill. His argument is that the quality of voice transmission will be such that it won't be necessary to write; we will speak our ideas, and they will be transmitted and documented in perfectly satisfactory ways. That may happen someday. Maybe even in this century.

But not now.

For now, writing well remains an essential skill for business success. I'm not talking about elegant, poetic writing, but clearly constructed and convincing written prose. Business writing is actually a bit of a unique genre, and one that not all schools teach. The closest comparison may be journalism, because the key to writing well for business (as in journalism) is to get the critical points first and then add supporting information. Always remember that many readers may not go beyond your first paragraph if it isn't compelling.

Good writing is essential not only in formal reports or proposals but also in your everyday communications (see "Impress Them with E-mail").

One recent assessment concluded that more than 50 percent of students at four-year schools and more than 75 percent at two-year colleges lacked the skills to perform complex literacy tasks. This means that they could not interpret data in a table, could not understand the arguments of newspaper editorials, could not compare credit card offers with different interest rates and annual fees, and could not summarize the results

impress them with e-mail

Develop your written communication skills to the highest level, both in your daily e-mails and in deliverables (assigned work documents) for which you are responsible. This includes correct grammar, capitalization, and punctuation—even in e-mail.

Why it works: if you can quickly fire off sharp e-mails, you will come across as highly capable and intelligent (provided your content isn't inappropriate). Not everyone types well, and certainly not everyone writes well.

Today, many first impressions are made through e-mail. If you present well there, you will develop your personal brand, and when people are surprised by how young you are compared with what they expected, you will know that you've already broken some of their preconceptions about your generation.[a]

a. Chuck Westbrook, "6 Ways to Get Respect Quickly, Despite Your Youth," August 6, 2007, http://www.employeeevolution.com/archives/2007/08/06/6-ways-to-get-respect-quickly-despite-your-youth/.

of a survey into a clear and understandable paragraph. The assessment revealed deficits in two types of literacy: interpreting information accurately and expressing arguments in a cogent, persuasive way.[2]

Lack of these skills is a serious shortcoming for your generation as you enter the corporate world. You must read and write well—by business standards.

writing in business

Is there a straightforward way to improve? Yes, through the application of the *pyramid principle.*[3] This simple approach, originally codified by consulting firm McKinsey & Company and taught to all its associates, has spread widely among business communicators because it is a logical, straightforward way to get your points across as convincingly as possible.

The first step is to identify four things:

- ✓ **Situation:** What is the issue (e.g., thinking and communicating clearly are essential to business success)?

- ✓ **Complication:** Why are you even addressing this issue? What's wrong (e.g., many Y's don't do it particularly well)?

- ✓ **Question:** What are you trying to figure out (e.g., is there a straightforward way to improve?)?

- ✓ **Answer:** What is the solution (e.g., yes, through the application of the pyramid principle)?

This last point is a big deal: note that you provide your answer right up front! Not after a meandering buildup, not through the suspenseful parsing out of facts (as you might if you were writing a novel), but at the beginning.

To back up your answer—which may, in fact, be the conclusion of your analysis or the recommendation you are making—you should then list your *supporting arguments* in as crisp and clear a way as possible (e.g., the pyramid principle has been used effectively for many years in many business situations, and it is easy to learn).

Here's another example. Let's assume that you want to write a memo to your boss requesting funding to set up a home office and permission to work from home at certain times during the week. Write a crisp message, structured around these five points of logic.

- ✓ My work involves a significant amount of time spent conducting analyses and writing, both of which require uninterrupted stretches of concentration. *(Situation)*

- ✓ The office environment is filled with frequent, distracting conversations and meetings. *(Complication)*

- ✓ I have sought an option that makes good business sense and would allow me to be more productive. *(Question you have addressed)*

- ✓ I recommend that I work from home three days a week. *(Answer)*

- ✓ I would have more time for my key tasks of analysis and writing. I have calculated that I spend an average of three hours each day in meetings or in hallway conversations; by coming in two days a week, I would still have an adequate level of face-to-face interaction. *(Supporting points)*

Clearly when you actually write the memo itself, you won't include the labels "situation" and the like, but do use the logic of that structure as you prepare a short, to-the-point message.

Lay out your thoughts in a logical and persuasive way. Give your ideas their best shot to be understood and accepted.

reason, reason is my middle name: logic

Business runs on logic—*financial* logic. If you are going to succeed in business in any capacity, you need to understand something about finance. I won't let you off the hook on this one
because you think you're going into a role that isn't "financial."
All roles in business are financial. Every single one.

If you want to succeed, you need to be able to do three financial things:

✓ You must understand how your company makes money
   and understand the regular reports your company
   releases about its performance.

✓ You must monitor the context—what's happening in the
   world that influences your business's future.

✓ You must be able to express your ideas in the language
   of business. You must give people *reasons* for your
   actions or suggestions that tie in to bottom-line
   financial terms.

Don't miss out on having your ideas accepted because people
don't immediately understand your logic. In business, make
reason your middle name.[4]

understand how your company makes money

You need to learn basic financial terms and observe how they
are used within your firm. At a minimum, you should know the
following things about your business:

✓ **Revenue:** How much money does the company get from selling products or services to customers? To whom does it sell goods and services? What are the major sources of the money your company takes in? Which sources are the most important? Which are the fastest growing? Why do customers buy your products or services? What is your company's strategy for getting them to buy more? How does your job contribute to that strategy?

✓ **Expense:** What does it cost your company to produce its products or deliver its services? What are the other costs associated with operating the business, including administrative expenses, employee salaries, rents, and sales and marketing costs? Which costs are most significant? How do the expenses relate to your company's strategy for getting customers to buy more of your products or services? How does your job contribute to managing the costs?

✓ **Profit:** What is left over after the expenses are subtracted from the revenue? There are a number of terms commonly used to track profit: operating income, EBIT (earnings before interest and tax), EBITDA (earnings before interest, taxes, depreciation, and amortization), and so on. Which term or terms does your company use, and what exactly does it mean? What is included in the calculation?

Find out which reports or other sources of information your company uses to share its financial results with employees. Are there regular reports that you may have access to? Are there teleconferences or town hall–type meetings with management? Be sure to access this information, and, if there are terms used that you don't understand, don't hesitate to ask a colleague to explain them to you. No one will think less of you for admitting you don't know, and they will be pleased that you are interested in learning more.

understand the world that influences your business's future

Become familiar with the key issues that could affect your business. Who are your key competitors, and how are they doing? Are there important government regulations or financial institutions that affect your business? Is a significant part of your company's business conducted in other countries, and, if so, what current events are happening in those areas? Is your business affected by any particular metric, such as the consumer confidence index, the number of housing starts, or interest rates?

Regularly read relevant publications, such as the *Wall Street Journal*, the *Economist*, and other business publications.

express your ideas in the language of business

Be able to discuss whether the proposals or suggestions you are making are worth the investment of time and money that would be required. Never take a suggestion forward without considering whether or not it (the investment of time or money required) would be worth it (the benefit you anticipate would result). Few things will make you look inexperienced faster than recommending something that is ridiculously out of balance (far more expensive or time consuming than it's worth in terms of any reasonable value that you might expect to receive).

The most difficult part of expressing your ideas this way is often simply determining what the investments and, particularly, what the returns might be in financial terms. Doing this much—developing a reasonable estimate of the associated costs and likely financial results—will dramatically strengthen your argument even if you don't go on to the second step of calculating the actual returns.

Making a list of the required investments should not be too difficult, but be sure to consider time as well as specific monetary investments. In business, time is money. So, for example, the cost of installing a new piece of machinery might include the following:

✓ The cost of buying the machine itself.

✓ The cost of the labor required for installation.

✓ The cost of disposing of the old machine, perhaps, or otherwise preparing the site.

✓ The cost of downtime while people are not working as the machine is being installed (assuming it occurs during work hours). You need to come up with a reasonable way to translate this into costs, such as the average per hour wage cost or the lost revenue of products that would have been built during that time.

A more difficult challenge for most people is to compose a reasonable summary of the likely results of the investment. Often people stop at what business calls *soft benefits*: employees will be happier, the quality of the product will be greater, the delivery time will be shorter, the flexibility to produce customized products will be greater. These are all terrific results, but you need to push yourself to quantify them. So, for example, happier employees might mean that retention rates would be higher and the cost of recruiting and training new employees would be lower. Higher product quality might mean that sales would increase. You can estimate the financial value of these latter items.

You don't need to have historic data to validate your assumptions (although if you do, that's great). All you need are reasonable *ifs*. You can present your estimates as follows: "We expect that this investment will increase employee satisfaction. If we assume that higher satisfaction reduces turnover by 10 percent," (choose the lowest *if* you can—make sure it seems *very* reasonable) "the cost savings in reduced recruiting and training expenses will be . . . "

Learning to speak in business language in terms of investment costs and estimated returns doesn't require an MBA or even a course in finance—only common sense and the discipline to keep going until you get to an end result that can be translated into financial terms.

investment costs and estimated returns: lay out the FACTS of your case

To develop the estimated costs and likely financial results associated with a project in a systematic way, lay out the FACTS (facts, assumptions, costs, timing, sensitivities). Identify the following:

✓ **Facts:** Information (data) on the current situation.

✓ **Assumptions:** Your estimate of how this investment would improve the current situation, translated into financial terms. Remember that you may need to go through several layers of logic to get to benefits that you can assign a financial value to: happier employees means higher retention, which means lower recruiting and training costs. Now you can assign a financial value.

✓ **Costs:** The amount of cash you will need to invest.

✓ **Timing:** How the costs and benefits will occur over time (how much each year).

✓ **Sensitivities:** Elements of your analysis that are uncertain and would significantly affect the outcome. You may want to redo your analysis several times, varying these assumptions, or at least be prepared to answer questions about why you think they are not likely to occur.

Now, try it for yourself; lay out the FACTS for purchasing new equipment from the information in "The FACTS for Purchasing New Equipment."

Accompanying your ideas with even a simple assessment of the financial investments and returns shows that you have thought through the reason for your recommendations or suggestions and that you've mastered the basic business finance language and logic. So don't be intimidated; use this approach to implement your recommendations and ideas in your organization.

the FACTS for purchasing new equipment

Use this set of information to walk through a FACTS evaluation for yourself:

— Your company is considering buying a specialized piece of equipment that will double your production capacity.

— It's expected to last three years.

— At the end of *each* one of the three years, the incremental cash flow from increased sales is estimated at $1,300.

Check your analysis against mine in table 11-1.

TABLE 11-1

Example: The FACTS for purchasing new equipment

Fact	Cash flow from current sales are $1,300 per year.
Assumption	The new equipment would double capacity and last three years.
	We can sell as much product as we can produce, and therefore the extra capacity will translate into higher sales.
Costs	The new equipment would cost $3,000, including the cost of installation.
	Installation will occur at night and will not disrupt current production.

Timing

Year 0	Year 1	Year 2	Year 3	Year 4	Year 5
(3,000)	$1,300	$1,300	$1,300		

Sensitivities (and other anticipated questions)	The market might not be there for more product: what if the incremental cash flow were only $1,000 per year?
	The equipment might last longer than three years: what if its life expectancy were five years?

12. business finesse— soft skills for tangible results

If you're not yet in the work world, then much of what you've been evaluated on is *content*—the ability to master specific areas of knowledge or expertise and your skill in developing concrete solutions or concepts or in performing defined tasks well. When it comes to content, the criteria are pretty clear for measuring whether your performance is better than someone else's performance.

In the work world, you begin to be evaluated increasingly on *process*—your ability to make things happen, to get things done. Being "right" becomes less important than being effective (and right, of course—clearly you don't want to get the wrong things done!). Success requires what are often called *soft skills*, or interpersonal skills: the ability to persuade and influence others.

For many people, one of the frustrating elements of transitioning from school to work is letting go of a focus on being right and shifting to being effective.

As you move to more senior roles in organizations—or start your own—your role will expand again. The leaders of organizations are responsible for what I call *context*—creating environments in which others can excel at getting the right things done. Setting the context, even more than being effective, requires strong soft skills.

This chapter looks at eight soft skills that are particularly important for Y's. Some of them capitalize on your generation's strengths, and others address common pitfalls. Of course, not every reader of this book needs to improve the strengths or overcome the challenges highlighted here. But even if you're already on top of your game, I hope this chapter will provide some useful reminders of timeless strategies for success.

The first three tips leverage several of your generation's best shared characteristics: optimism, initiative, and learning.

✓ **Think positively:** The power of optimism and confidence

✓ **Why not do it yourself?** The excitement of initiative

✓ **Make the most of it:** The ability to turn learning into luck

The next three tips will help you counteract some common misperceptions about your generation. Use them to avoid the traps others may expect you will fall into: being insensitive to the existing realities of a situation, depending on your parents or others to intervene on your behalf, or avoiding direct face-to-face interaction because you are so accustomed to communicating via technology.

✓ **It has to work for the other guy:** The benefits of pragmatism

✓ **Walk fast, carry a stack of papers, and drink coffee:** The importance of being perceived as purposeful

✓ **Clear the air and move on:** The satisfaction of direct discussions—and letting go

The final two are in some ways timeless suggestions—important for every generation. They support and amplify values that I know are important to most of you. Leverage both fully as you enter the world of work.

✓ **Do the hula:** The role of grace under pressure

✓ **Keep three months' salary in the bank:** The freedom to walk away

As you enter the work world, you face choices about how to interact every single day—how to mesh your expectations and preferences with whatever reality you find. On one hand, you could adapt fully to the old rules of corporate life. On the other, you could push back sharply. I'm advocating a middle road: that you challenge the "what," but do so in a way that is smart and respectful and that recognizes how corporations work today. You also need to share what you know in ways that help corporations evolve in directions that will be important to their success going forward.

In this chapter, I talk about some of the "hows"—ways that work to get things done in corporations. Following these practices will help you be seen for your contributions rather than your age, get noticed more quickly, and earn greater influence and responsibility. They will help you create change in the corporations you join.

think positively: the power of optimism and confidence

Norman Vincent Peale, a motivational speaker popular in the 1950s and 1960s, spoke fervently about the "power of positive thinking." I love the phrase—and its lesson for business. There is tremendous power in optimism and confidence. A lot of what happens in any organization happens because the person advocating a course of action or a particular position exudes confidence and energy about the choice. That confidence draws others in.

For much of my career I've worked as a consultant to management teams in corporations throughout the United States, Europe, Asia, and the Middle East. Without intending to sound disrespectful to the profession, I believe good consulting can be characterized by a serious pun: it is the ultimate "con" game— by which I mean not *con* in the sense of pulling something over on some unsuspecting soul, but in the sense that what good consultants provide to their clients, ultimately, is *confidence*.

Rarely, if ever, have I been in a situation when the idea I presented was totally new, never before considered. Instead, what I have helped many leadership teams do is align themselves with confidence behind one of the options that they had already known existed. The value I've delivered is confidence.

Some of it comes from analysis, and some of it, particularly as I've gotten more experienced, comes from my own confidence that the action I'm recommending is the best one for my client.

Happily, most of you start out with a healthy dose of self-confidence and self-esteem. Don't lose it—use it!

Unfortunately, maintaining a sense of confidence, or certainly a sense of being special, in some ways runs counter to the fundamental philosophy of industrial age corporations. Many corporate policies stress the importance of treating everyone the same—removing the specialness of any one individual. In addition, the metrics that you've grown accustomed to—grades, being right—are not what counts in business.

Listen to Lyn Chamberlin, author of Being Good Is Not Enough:

> *"This is a wake-up call to all current and just-graduated students. And the message is simple: Being good is no longer enough. Your 3.9 GPA, varsity soccer, three-language proficiency, year in South America, work-study in the campus bookstore, volunteering at the homeless shelter, bylines in the school paper, interning every summer since you stopped going to camp are simply not going to haul the water no matter what your parents, your advisor or the career service administrator tells you. From this moment on, it's all up to you."[1]*

You need to maintain your confidence despite any buffeting you may take as you swim in unfamiliar waters. And even though confidence is a mental attitude that will grow as you become more plugged in to your work and workplace experience, there are a few tricks that can support you as you develop it.

First, *appearing* confident counts, and, at the most obvious level, that translates into appearing appropriately put together. Emerging from the often hypercritical teenage years, you know the importance of appearances. The key to appearing appropriate for business is no different from what it was then: take your cues from what others are wearing (see "Common Clothes Sense").

I had an advantage: the hot book when I graduated from business school was *Dress for Success*, a compendium of unequivocal rules for proper appearance in the corporate world.[2] Millions of us devoured it, eager to gain every possible compet-

common clothes sense

Linen suits look good only in the J.Crew catalog. The rest of the world wears wool.

Don't blow all your graduation money on a new work wardrobe. Wait until you've settled into your job, collected a paycheck or two, and observed what others are wearing.

If you have to ask yourself, "Is this appropriate for my office?" then it probably isn't.

If you're unsure of the dress code, ask. No one wants you dressed like an Easter egg in front of a client.

Dressing like a professional makes you feel like a professional. And do you really want to be mistaken for an intern during happy hour? Dress accordingly.[a]

a. Susan Johnston, "What Not to Wear to Work," June 11, 2007. http://www.brazencareerist.com/author/susan-johnston

itive advantage. To this day, I have never worn a brown suit in Boston.

Fortunately, there's no need to be so tightly restricted today. Unfortunately, there's also no clear formula to ensure that you don't show up looking out of place. You need to pay attention to what others are wearing, and, if in doubt, ask. You don't want to show up in a suit and tie if jeans are the norm—and certainly not the reverse.

But appearing confident goes far beyond the clothes you wear. It includes the amount of preparation you've done and the way you react to new challenges.

One of the worst mistakes you can make is to signal to an audience or an individual you're meeting with that you haven't given your project the attention it deserves. Even if you feel you could have done more, sound as if you're fully in control. I witnessed a colleague shoot himself in the foot by beginning a speech in front of a huge crowd of senior executives by saying, "I put these thoughts together this morning on my way here." He lost the audience with that opening. He was implying that he had not bothered to work on his remarks for more than a few minutes the morning of his speech. The people in the audience felt they were unimportant to him. In truth, I suspect he was very nervous and hoping that such an opening would gain sympathy from the audience, but that's not the way it works. Sound confident—and prepared.

Be sure to react with calm when new assignments are first described to you. Here's one of the practical ways this will come into play. Almost inevitably, you'll be in a situation (probably many times) in which someone will ask you to do something that you have absolutely no idea how to do. Ask questions about *what* to be sure you understand exactly what output is desired, but don't get into a detailed discussion about *how*, at least not initially. Look confident, go away, and figure out how to do it or at least what the options are for doing it. If you need to check back on the *how*, go back with specific questions ("Would you prefer that I approach it like this or like that?"). Exude confidence, and you will be given even more interesting challenges to tackle.

why not do it yourself?
the excitement of initiative

Although I loved many things about the management consulting company I joined after graduate school, there were also many times when I felt frustrated. As at most big companies, the number of processes that seemed hopelessly bureaucratic and the ripe opportunities that appeared to go begging seemed staggering. Why on earth didn't someone deal with that?

One day, the obvious realization sank in: why don't *I* deal with it myself?

Hmm, why indeed?

Whenever you hear yourself thinking, "Why doesn't *someone. . .* " consider whether it might be possible to do it yourself. Take on responsibility for making your firm a better place— more successful in the market or more engaging in the work environment. Don't complain without also offering constructive suggestions and expressing the willingness to do the work required to make the improvements happen. Don't be afraid to step into a leadership vacuum. Here are three strengths you can bring to the task:[3]

✓ Look for new and better ways to do things, starting with the specific tasks you've been hired to do. Do your own work smarter, and share your improvements with colleagues. For example, you might create templates for common tasks or write scripts or standard e-mails for common customer interactions. Find ways to get more done in less time. In the end, intelligent managers will be delighted. There aren't many companies that don't appreciate bottom-line results.

✓ You can demonstrate leadership by helping other employees be more effective. Be generous: help others format documents, create spreadsheets, or find information on the Web. Answer questions for fellow Gen Y's. Introduce older colleagues to some of the time-saving technologies you may use. If you have workers of every age looking to you to be more effective, you'll have their respect by default.

✓ You are more likely than many of your older colleagues to have the skills required to lead even without the blessings of hierarchical authority. Use your Gen Y knowledge of how to network, build relationships, use influence, and work with others to achieve the results you seek. Attract people by sharing ownership and building a community of ideas.

There's one important corollary to the lesson of taking initiative: first, do what you've committed to do—and do it well. One of the big mistakes people make is to assume that taking on a new project, even one that is widely viewed as useful and important, somehow excuses falling short on their original objectives. That is rarely true. If you are going to volunteer to tackle a new issue—or if someone asks you whether you have time to tackle a new issue—make sure you ask yourself, "Will I be able to do this *and* meet my original objectives?" New ideas don't let you off the hook of meeting your existing commitments.

make the most of it: the ability to turn learning into luck

The ability to get something useful out of virtually any situation is one of the great skills of successful people. If you're talking to someone who describes a seemingly negative situation or experience but regards it as a positive lesson learned, you're probably talking with a "lucky" person.

Learning is probably the best way to make the most of an otherwise less-than-great situation. So even if you get momentarily stuck in a company or position you don't like, challenge yourself to see how much learning you can draw out of the experience. This should be a natural for you: your top workplace values are "the growth potential" in a position (55 percent) and "intellectual stretch" (49 percent).[4]

Start by being curious about how the business operates. Can you see any ways for improvement? I'm always a bit impatient with people who tell me they're bored; it tells me that they're not using their imagination to look at what they can draw out of the situation. I had a part-time job in college working on the production line in a book bindery—truly one of the most routine and potentially boring jobs possible. But I had a great time. Thinking about the steps in the process, ways they might be made easier, and other improvement ideas kept me well occupied throughout my hours at work, and I ended up making a useful contribution to the company in the end.

Spend time getting to know your older colleagues and picking their brains for ideas. One of the best ways to learn within most corporations is by leveraging the skills and knowledge of older workers who are willing to share what they know before they retire.[5] Many Y's are recognizing the value of experienced workers' knowledge and using them as sources of advice and instruction. Seek advice from people with a good reputation and the right experience.

Also, get to know people up the chain of command. Take advantage of any opportunities to interact with upper management. Participate in forums, question-and-answer sessions, and special project groups, and don't be shy about introducing yourself at the proper moment. You'll find that in many cases, your boss's boss's boss is a very cool person with a lot to share.[6] If you approach these interactions looking to see how much you can learn from the older person (rather than how smart you can make yourself appear), it's likely to be a success on both counts.

it has to work for the other guy: the benefits of pragmatism

This lesson originally came from a man who was a hotshot when I was a low-level bag carrier at that management consulting firm. From my vantage point, he was pretty full of himself, but he was also darn good: articulate, bright—a real star. One day, he surprised me by admitting that his early assignments had been largely a disaster. He had focused his early work on coming up with the "best" possible answer—brilliant, logical, well supported, irrefutable—just what would have earned him high marks in school. But none of his clients had accepted his recommendations. No one implemented any of his work, and none of the clients hired him for a second job.

Finally, he figured out that what really mattered was how well his recommendations *worked for the other guy*—in this case, for the client organizations that he had been hired to advise.

Success in business is not about having the most brilliant answer. It is not even necessarily about being "right." It's about making things work—and that means developing a really good understanding of the organization you're trying to affect and the people you're trying to convince. You need to get away from thinking like a student (*I have the right answer*) to thinking like a businessperson (*I can help make this work*). To do this, you need to be really tuned in to what some call politics and what my colleagues and I often call the organization's *hidden logic*.

hidden logic: decode the unwritten rules

Every organization has codes of conduct, ways of operating that are not immediately apparent—unwritten rules of the game. Here's how to understand the hidden logic in your organization.[7]

First, listen carefully to the advice that experienced members of the organization share. Pay particular attention to the exact language they use to express their sense of how things work. Figures 12-1, 12-2, and 12-3 show how the buzzwords you might hear in three different organizations relate to the behavior you're likely to experience. Can you imagine how different life in each organization is likely to be?

FIGURE 12-1

The hidden logic of Blue Company: Take care of yourself

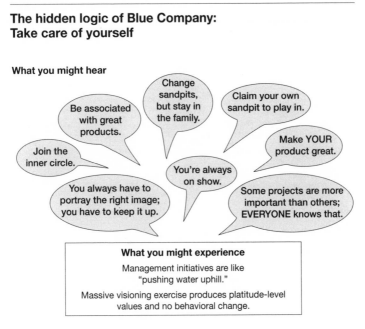

What you might hear

- Be associated with great products.
- Change sandpits, but stay in the family.
- Claim your own sandpit to play in.
- Join the inner circle.
- Make YOUR product great.
- You're always on show.
- You always have to portray the right image; you have to keep it up.
- Some projects are more important than others; EVERYONE knows that.

> **What you might experience**
>
> Management initiatives are like "pushing water uphill."
>
> Massive visioning exercise produces platitude-level values and no behavioral change.

Source: Peter Scott-Morgan, "Hidden Logic Imperative," The Concours Group (now nGenera), January 1, 2005.

Second, group what you hear into one of three categories:

✓ **Motivators:** What is *really* important to people?

It's important to understand motivators and use them as ways of showing how your ideas will help support these goals. But they are usually difficult to change. If you're suggesting something that is contrary to your colleagues' motivators, you're facing a long, uphill struggle.

FIGURE 12-2

The hidden logic of Red Company: Keep your head down

What you might hear

What you might experience

Very difficult to give negative feedback
(hurtful, you're viewed as "mean" or aggressive).

Easy to rationalize "hiding" bad news.

Source: Peter Scott-Morgan, "Hidden Logic Imperative," The Concours Group (now nGenera), January 1, 2005.

✓ **Enablers:** Who is important?

Enablers can be changed, of course, although it may require significant time and effort.

✓ **Triggers:** How and when do things happen?

Triggers are usually the easiest of the three to change with modest investments of time and energy.

So, for example, let's say that you are charged with leading an innovation team within White Company that requires the combined skills and expertise of people from several divisions.

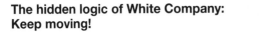

FIGURE 12-3

The hidden logic of White Company:
Keep moving!

What you might hear

Don't get near an effort that might fail—keep your "no failure" track record clean.

Job hop as quickly as possible—the most successful people have a record of changing every 18 months or less.

Focus on earning that next promotion.

Deliver your quarter-to-quarter results at all costs.

Keep your boss—and your boss's boss—happy.

The solid line relationships are the ones that do the reviews and pay the money; don't worry about the dotted lines.

At the end of the day, you will be judged and rewarded based on your ability to run your territory.

Control is a big thing around here; we fight a lot.

Protect your own turf.

The culture is impacting the rate of change.

What you might experience
Poor teamwork, no synergy, short-term thinking, no creative risk taking.

Source: Peter Scott-Morgan, "Hidden Logic Imperative," The Concours Group (now nGenera), January 1, 2005.

That would be a tough challenge, based on the way the hidden logic works at the moment. Rather than jumping in and trying to push your initiative through, step back and think about how you might make the system work with you, rather than against you, as it almost surely will as currently structured.

✓ **What motivates people in White Company?**
Promotions.

✓ **Who enables actions in White Company?** Each person's immediate boss and boss's boss.

✓ **What are the important triggers?** Quarterly results within your immediate sphere of responsibility and a "no failure" track record.

So, what are your options? You need to address the triggers. You need to make sure that participation on your team will be an important part of each person's evaluation, and you need to make sure that taking risks—and potentially failing—will be seen as a plus, not a minus. You might address this by working to have participation on a cross-divisional team formally added to the promotion criteria. You might see whether it would be possible for you to become one of the enablers (in other words, to have significant input into the person's promotion decision). Or you might seek other similar approaches to address the issue. The point is, don't fight the hidden logic. Instead, work with it to have maximum impact.

Lay out the organization's hidden logic in a systematic way, and consider where it is likely to thwart the initiatives you're trying to lead and how you can either leverage or rewrite the rules to make them work for you.[8]

Asking your colleagues questions about how things work—what's important to them, who's important to various decisions, and what causes various things to happen—is a sign of good organizational sense, not of weakness or inability. You'll learn the culture more efficiently and develop better insights into how to get your ideas across.[9]

Your ideas will get implemented. You'll help make things work.

walk fast, carry a stack of papers, and drink coffee: the importance of being perceived as purposeful

My first boss at my precollege job, the weekly newspaper, was ink-stained and perpetually harried as he raced from meeting to meeting, up and down Main Street and back to the presses in time for each week's mad race to publication. He gave me what might have been my single most useful piece of advice on how to succeed in business: "Walk fast—and always carry a stack of papers and a cup of coffee."

I've followed that advice ever since.

Of course, what he was really saying was to appear purposeful: look as if you know what you're doing and where you're headed. Give people the impression that you're doing something that has a sense of urgency and perhaps importance, and act as if you're totally alert and plugged in to what's going on around you.

Most organizations have a low tolerance for people who waffle. It's fine not to know the answer, but it's not fine to take up everyone else's time expressing your uncertainty. If you don't know what you need to know, ask smart questions and figure out how to get it. Being resourceful and self-sufficient—being purposeful—is a very good thing.

Short of that, appearing so is the next best thing. I'd love to tell you that you will be judged solely on your tangible contributions, your merits alone. You won't. Perceptions count, just as my newspaper boss advised.

Y's face a rather unusual challenge in appearing self-sufficient: your well-meaning parents. I know that your parents' well-intentioned efforts on your behalf are one side of what is a close relationship. As I've discussed in earlier chapters, most of you genuinely like and respect your parents. It's natural and understandable that you would turn to them for support.

Asking for advice is great. You may also be able to rehearse key presentations with them. And you might ask them to hold you accountable—to serve as a career coach—meeting with you regularly, discussing progress, and helping you shape new ideas.

But in the work environment, you've got to stand on your own. Period. Parental support and advice are good, but your organization will—and should—see only *your* decisions and actions. Draw the line at anything that would detract from your employer's sense of your self-reliance, anything that would make you appear less purposeful.

Carry your own cup of coffee.

clear the air and move on: the satisfaction of direct discussions—and letting go

Even with the most astute understanding of the organization and the greatest ideas, there will be times when you're not going to agree—or even get along—with some of your colleagues. This tip is about how you can air disagreements and address difficult issues face-to-face.

In the workplace, it is critical to address issues openly and constructively, even if they're difficult. In most cases, there is no option for picking up your toys and going home (unless you plan to leave the organization). Instead, you need to make the relationships you've been dealt, work.

Here's the key: candor is never the problem. People never become defensive about what you say directly to them. People become defensive because of *why* they think you're saying it, and they certainly become very defensive if they find out that you didn't say anything at all (or said it behind their back).

There are three steps to holding a difficult conversation, particularly one in which you need to confront a point of disagreement: the preparation you do before the conversation, the way you arrange to hold the conversation, and the follow-up afterward.[10]

1. **Preparation before:** Start by assuming good intentions on the part of the other person. Try to identify as many rational reasons that he might have for his position. Ask yourself three questions.

   - I wonder why a reasonable, rational, and decent person might do or think that?

   - What could I imagine *might* be happening? Could it be motivation? Or ability?

   - Were other people or things involved?

   Adopting a generous, open-minded attitude is probably the single most important part of holding successful conversations.

2. **During the conversation:** Make the conversation feel safe for the other person. Be respectful and, if the conversation is in any way sensitive, request to speak in private. Ask the other person's permission to discuss the topic at hand, and establish that you have a mutual

purpose—a common interest in addressing the issue satisfactorily.

Right up front, address the other person's possible concerns that you don't respect him or that you have a malicious intent, and clarify your real purpose for the conversation: "I don't want you to think I'm saying that I can't count on you. I find you to be quite reliable. I do, however, have concerns over what happened with your most recent assignment."

Throughout the conversation, link your points to the other individual's values. Always end the conversation with a question to confirm that he is aligned with the outcome, and agree on who will follow up in what way, when, and where.

3. **Following up after the conversation:** Follow up! Meet with the person again to ensure that you are both meeting your agreed-upon commitments.

   And debrief. Ask yourself whether there would be ways to be more effective next time:

   – Did I pick the right problem to discuss?

   – Was I open to a variety of possibilities?

   – Was I respectful?

   – Did I link my concerns to her values and purpose?

   – Did we agree on a specific plan?

Don't make your colleagues guess your intentions or concerns. Be open and clear. And when difficult issues surface, tackle them head on, with respect and confidence.

do the hula: the role of grace under pressure

I have to warn you: the odds are that you'll find yourself in some awkward and uncomfortable situations over the course of your career—ones you wish you could wiggle out of. I know I have.

Have you ever attended one of those stage shows where they drag some poor unsuspecting audience members up on stage? I was at one where they tied a grass skirt around two guys' waists and encouraged them both to do the hula. Clearly neither one was thrilled, but they reacted in very different ways. One resisted, protested, squirmed, and basically refused to play along. He came off looking ridiculous. The other guy pasted on a smile, gritted his teeth, and did the hula. He looked like a champ.

There will be lots of times in business when you find yourself, figuratively, with a grass skirt tied around your waist—assignments that don't match your skills, clients who are making unreasonable demands, truly embarrassing social moments. Of course, it's always fine to demur initially, to let people know that you'd prefer not to do whatever. But there will inevitably come times when you are in the situation with no obvious route of escape.

So, do the hula, with grace. Grit your teeth and give it your very best. Try to knock the ball out of the park. The worst thing you can do at that point would be to squirm and complain. Throw yourself into it. Your "good sport" attitude won't be forgotten.

keep three months' salary in the bank: the freedom to walk away

This final piece of advice is from Raymond Corey, my favorite professor at business school. He taught marketing, but his parting words to us were about the ability to walk away.

He encouraged us to keep enough money in the bank at all times to have the confidence to walk away from any job. He urged us to make sure we would never feel we had to stay in an untenable situation only for the money. His argument was based primarily on a concern for corporate ethics; he wanted us to avoid working for any firm whose ethical standards were below our own (prophetic wisdom in those pre-Enron days).

I suggest taking Professor Corey's advice one step further—beyond ethics to the broader ability to take risks. I think you do your best work when you feel that you could quit your job at any time if you had to. Your choice of when to follow the rules and when to push back is based on a smart analysis of the situation (the hidden logic, the types of open conversations you need to have) rather than on a fear that you must toe the line at all costs. Lance Armstrong said, commenting on how cancer was instrumental in his ability to win the Tour de France, "I could go out without risk—it was all upside."[11]

You'll do the job better if you feel your options are all upside.

. . . . .

Corporations need you. They are struggling to learn to operate effectively in a networked, collaborative world. They are facing a shortage of talented people. They are looking for innovative ideas, including products and services that will connect with choice-oriented consumers. You have a lot to offer.

But talent alone is not enough. To make the most of your talent, you have to plug in to your workplace, to connect with the people, to get your ideas across in ways that are compelling, and to address potential roadblocks in constructive ways.

Practice these skills. As you do, your capabilities will grow materially. Soon you'll be ready to make a new impression— you'll be doing something that will trigger your coworkers to take out their cameras. Each new picture will reflect a new step in your contribution to the world of work.

conclusion

I hope I'm not giving away any major secret here. I'm taking a gamble that any of you who planned to see the movie or read the book *The Devil Wears Prada* have already done so.

Bottom line: she doesn't take the promotion.

Andrea, the movie's Gen Y protagonist, works *so* very hard to pursue her dream job. She jumps into an industry with which she has little familiarity and with no discernible qualifications. She rises to almost impossible challenges, tackling arduous tasks with ingenuity and boundless energy. She relies in part on the wise coaching of a Boomer colleague and skirts the deep resentment of a Gen X'er who feels passed over. In the end, she succeeds in meeting the extraordinarily exacting standards of her over-the-top, competitive Boomer boss.

Then, on the brink of even greater success, she quits.

OK, she has also sacrificed true love and lasting friendships in pursuit of her professional goal, but—let me emphasize—she *won!*

And she quit.

Now, let's 'fess up. What did you think of that ending?

I feel safe in suggesting that many Boomers found the ending, well . . . astonishing—and to some, honestly, ridiculous. Why would you work so hard and not take advantage of winning? If Andrea had stayed in the job and enjoyed the spoils of success, that would make sense. Perhaps she might even have changed the corporate culture for the better, serving as a humane role model for the next trainee. But to quit while she was ahead? Please.

In contrast, most X'ers like the ending. The pinnacle Andrea had reached in the corporate world was, after all, clearly unstable. Yes, she was on top—today—but, if nothing else, the movie had made it obvious that being up one day in no way guaranteed a place tomorrow. Wise to get out now. One of my Gen X friends elaborated: "For X'ers, the movie is about what's wrong with organizations and why it's a mistake to hitch your wagon to any one person or any one organization for too long or without a sense that the organization will love you back."

And most of you? Well, most of the Y's I've asked *love* the ending. The heroine rose to the challenge, learned a lot, and then moved on to find something that struck a deeper chord in her soul. One of my Gen Y friends explained: "For me, although obviously there was some suspense, I knew going in that she had to decline the job—that's just what a Y would do. It was just a matter of how."

Although extreme, this movie may be more of a parable for the workplace today than we would like to admit. Y's are entering the workforce with enthusiasm and confidence—and succeeding on many fronts. Many of you are finding Boomers a bit schizophrenic—warm mentors as well as off-the-wall corporate warriors. And many X'ers have not exactly welcomed you with open arms.

Many Y's are also, at best, agnostic in their commitment to a corporate career. Maybe you'll stay, or maybe you'll move on to other work environments that offer a new blend of learning, challenge, and life balance. The old inducements—more money, "winning"—hold much less appeal.

I hope this book has changed your perspectives just a little. Not about money or winning, but about your ability to connect with the workplace—to change it rather than leave it—as the movie heroine did. I hope it has given you useful thoughts about how to find an environment in the first place that you'll love enough to want to invest the time and energy to do just that.

The next great generation—that's a heady label, for sure, although one that you're fully up to wearing. You have a long life, a fresh perspective, the support of many, and the confidence to make wonderful things happen.

Plug in—and create the life that's right for you.

notes

Introduction

1. Barry Schwartz, *The Paradox of Choice: How More Is Less* (New York: Ecco, 2004).

2. Throughout the book, quotations from Y's are from focus groups conducted as part of Re.sults Project YE, *Engaging Today's Young Employees*, The Concours Institute (now nGenera), 2007.

3. My blog, "Across the Ages," is available at http://discussionleader.hbsp .com/erickson/.

4. For a broader discussion of issues facing Gen Y's in other countries and those headed into other job categories, I hope you'll post your comments and questions on my blog.

Chapter 1

1. Harris Interactive YouthPulse, 2006, http://www.harrisinteractive.com.

2. "Background on the Millennial Generation," Young Voter Strategies, a nonpartisan project of the Graduate School of Political Management at The George Washington University, February 2007.

3. *A Global Generation Gap: Adapting to a New World*, Pew Research Center, February 24, 2004; Yale Online, www.yaleonline.edu.

4. Ibid.; ibid.

5. Year 2030 statistic: Carrie Sturrock, "We're Living Longer—Is That a Good Thing?" *San Francisco Chronicle*, March 6, 2006, http://www.sfgate.com/cgi-bin/article.cgi?file=/c/a/2006/03/06/MNGICHJ8311.DTL; life span of 120 years: Bruce J. Klein, "This Wonderful Lengthening of Lifespan," *The Longevity Meme*, January 17, 2003, http://www.longevitymeme.org/articles.

6. "Life Expectancy at Birth, 65 and 85 Years of Age, by Sex and Race: United States, Selected Years 1900–2003 (LIFEX03a)." National Center for Health Statistics, http://209.217.72.34/aging/TableViewer/tableView.aspx?ReportId=357.

7. David Brooks, "The Odyssey Years," *New York Times*, October 9, 2007; "emerging adulthood" from Jeffrey Jensen Arnett, *Emerging Adulthood: The Winding Road from the Late Teens through the Twenties* (New York, Oxford: Oxford University Press, 2004).

8. Year 2000 statistic: Brooks, "The Odyssey Years"; today's: E. Fussell and F. Furstenberg, "The Transition to Adulthood During the 20th Century: Race, Nativity and Gender," Network on Transitions to Adulthood, 2004, MacArthur Foundation.

9. U.S. statistic: Nadira A. Hira, "Attracting the Twenty-Something Worker," *Fortune*, May 15, 2007; international: Arnett, *Emerging Adulthood*.

10. Emily Flynn Vencat, "Narcissists in Neverland," *Newsweek*, October 16, 2007.

11. Data in this paragraph from "Background on the Millennial Generation; "How Young People View Their Lives, Futures and Politics," Pew Research Center for the People and the Press, January 8, 2007.

12. Data in this paragraph from "2006 Education at a Glance: OECD Indicators"; Gary Orfield, ed., *Dropouts in America: Confronting the Graduation Rate Crisis* (Cambridge, MA: Harvard Education Press, 2004); "Dropouts in California: Confronting the Graduation Rate Crisis," Civil Rights Project, Harvard University, research report, 2006.

13. "Are They Really Ready to Work? Employers' Perspectives on the Basic Knowledge and Applied Skills of New Entrants to the 21st Century Workforce," published jointly by The Conference Board, Corporate Voices for Working Families, the Partnership for 21st Century Skills, and the Society for Human Resource Management, October 2006.

14. Cited in Deepak Ramachandran and Paul Artiuch, "Harnessing the Global N-Gen Talent Pool," New Paradigm Learning Corporation (now nGenera), July 2007.

15. Discussion of IITs in India: Anand Giridharadas, "In India's Higher Education, Few Prizes for 2nd Place," *International Herald Tribune*, November 26, 2006, www.iht.com/articles/2006/11/26/news/india.php?page=1; Gen Y

potential in rising economies: Ramachandran and Artiuch, "Harnessing the Global N-Gen Talent Pool."

16. Diana Farrell and Andrew Grant, "Addressing China's Looming Talent Shortage," McKinsey Global Institute, October 2005, www.mckinsey.com/mgi/reports/pdfs/China_talent/ChinaPerspective.pdf.

17. "The Emerging Global Labor Market, Part II: The Supply of Offshore Talent in Services," McKinsey Global Institute, June 2005, www.mckinsey.com/mgi/reports/pdfs/emerginggloballabormarket/Part2/MGI_supply_executive summary.pdf.

18. Undergraduate figures: "At Colleges, Women Are Leaving Men in the Dust," *New York Times*, July 9, 2006; graduate school figures: U.S. Department of Education Mini-digest of Education Statistics 2006.

19. Brooks, "The Odyssey Years."

20. From "Across the Ages," http://discussionleader.hbsp.com/erickson/.

21. "2006 Employee Review," Randstad Work Solutions, 2006.

Chapter 2

1. Greenberg Quinian Rosner/Polimetrix YouthMonitor, *Coming of Age in America, Part III*, January 2006, 3.

2. Survey conducted by the Higher Education Research Institute at the University of California at Los Angeles and cited in Sharon Jayson, "Generation Y Gets Involved," *USA Today*, October 23, 2006.

3. College Explorer Study conducted by Harris Interactive on behalf of Alloy Media + Marketing, 2002; Jayson, "Generation Y Gets Involved."

4. Sheila Kinkade and Christina Macy, *Our Time Is Now: Young People Changing the World* (New York: Pearson Foundation, 2005), 9.

5. Both quotations cited in Jayson, "Generation Y Gets Involved."

6. Scott Keeter, "Politics and the 'DotNet' Generation," Pew Research Center for the People & the Press, May 30, 2006.

7. *The New Employee/Employer Equation*, The Concours Group (now nGenera) and Age Wave, 2004.

8. Don Tapscott, *Growing Up Digital: The Rise of the Net Generation* (New York: McGraw Hill, 1998); and *Media Family: Electronic Media in the Lives of Infants, Toddlers, Preschoolers, and Their Parents*, Kaiser Family Foundation Survey, 2006.

9. "Schools Dial Up New Communications Plans," *eSchool News*, May 19, 2006, citing survey by Student Monitor LLC in 2006; "Cellphone-Only Use Growing Among Youths," *USA Today*, May 14, 2007, citing research by the Centers for Disease Control and Prevention.

10. "Schools Dial Up New Communications Plans"; and "Home Truths About Telecoms," *Economist*, June 7, 2007, citing research conducted by Stefana Broadbent, an anthropologist at the User Adoption Lab at Swisscom

11. Jupiter Research, quoted in "Getting Out the (Text) Message," *Investor's Business Daily*, April 20, 2007; and "Teens and Technology," Pew Internet & American Life Project, July 27, 2005.

12. Statistics on Internet use, mobile access, online purchasing, content creation, social networking, and the metaverse from the Pew Internet Project, http://www.pewinternet.org/PPF/r/231/report_display.asp (U.S. data); and John Geraci and Lisa Chen, "Meet the Global New Generation," report by New Paradigm Learning Corporation (now nGenera), 2007. Based on a survey fielded using the Harris Poll Online panel from April 5 to May 3, 2007, among 5,935 members of Generation Y, aged sixteen to twenty-nine years, in twelve countries (the United States, Canada, the United Kingdom, Germany, France, Spain, Mexico, Brazil, Russia, China, Japan, and India).

13. *Women in the Labor Force: A Databook*, 2006 edition, Bureau of Labor Statistics, BLS Report 996, 2006.

14. "Many Women at Elite Colleges Set Career Path to Motherhood," *New York Times*, September 20, 2005; and Sylvia Ann Hewlett and Carolyn Buck Luce, "Off-Ramps and On-Ramps: Keeping Talented Women on the Road to Success," *Harvard Business Review* (March 2005): 43–54.

15. "2005 National Study of Employers: Highlights of Findings," Families and Work Institute, 2005.

16. "The First Measured Century: The Other Way of Looking at American History," host/essayist Ben Wattenberg, Public Broadcasting System, 2000.

17. D. Baumrind, "Rearing Competent Children," in William Damon, *Child Development Today and Tomorrow* (San Francisco: Jossey-Bass, 1989), 349–378. The Western reverence for the young that has emerged over the past half-century is not necessarily shared in the East, which tends to revere its older generations. This is an important cultural difference between Y's reared in Asia and those who grew up in North America and Europe.

18. Dr. Peter Markiewicz, "Who's Filling Gen Y's Shoes?" Brand Channel .com, May 5, 2003, http://www.brandchannel.com/features_effect.asp?pf_id =156. (Quoting research conducted by Applied Research & Consulting LLC.)

19. Gallup poll cited in "The Good-News Generation," *U.S. News & World Report*, November 3, 2003.

20. Pamela Paul, "The PermaParent Trap," *Psychology Today*, September–October 2003, http://psychologytoday.com/articles/index.php?term=pto-2003 0902-000002&page=1.

21. Paul, "The PermaParent Trap"; and Re.sults Project YE, *Engaging Today's Young Employees*, 2007.

22. Re.sults Project YE, *Engaging Today's Young Employees: Strategies for the Millennials*, The Concours Institute (now nGenera), 2007, 15.

23. Ben Grill, quoted in "Teen Trends: Inside the Minds of Today's Teens," Partnership for a Drug-Free America, http://www.drugfree.org/Parent/Knowing/Teen_Trends; and poll by Experience Inc., quoted in "Attracting the Twenty-something Worker," *CNN Money*, May 15, 2007.

24. Quotation: Nadira A. Hira, "Attracting the Twentysomething Worker," *Fortune*, May 15, 2007; survey: Neil Howe and William Strauss, *Helicopter Parents in the Workplace*, New Paradigm Learning Corporation (now nGenera), November 2007.

25. Sharon Jayson, "'Helicopter' Parents Cross All Age, Social Lines," *USA Today*, April 3, 2007. See also the work of Patricia Somers, an associate professor of education at the University of Texas-Austin, whose analysis is based on more than fifty interviews with officials from ten four-year public universities across the United States.

26. Statistics: "Parent Involvement in the College Recruiting Process: To What Extent?" CERI Research Brief 2-2007; quote information: Barbara Rose, "Gen Y's Parents Staying at Helm," *Chicago Tribune*, April 23, 2007, http://www.chicagotribune.com/business/columnists/chi-0704210029apr23,0,2583512.column?coll=chi-business-hed.

27. "Parent Involvement in the College Recruiting Process," CERI Research.

28. Tara Weiss, "Are Parents Killing Their Kids' Careers?" *Forbes.com*, November 9, 1996, http://www.forbes.com/2006/11/08/leadership-careers-jobs-lead-careers-cx_tw_1109kids.html.

Chapter 3

1. Nadira A. Hira, "You Raised Them, Now Manage Them," *Fortune*, May 28, 2007.

2. "The World Is Your Oyster," *Economist*, October 5, 2006.

3. "Gen Y Shaped, Not Stopped, by Tragedy," *USA Today*, April 17, 2007.

4. "How Young People View Their Lives, Futures and Politics: A Portrait of Generation Next," The Pew Research Center for the People & the Press, January 9, 2007.

5. Quarterlifecrisis.com survey conducted in 2001 of 153 recent high school graduates, as quoted in Abby Wilner and David Singleton, *The Quarter-*

life Crisis: The N-Gen Transition to Adulthood (Toronto: New Paradigm Learning Corporation (now nGenera), 2007); Barry Schwartz, *The Paradox of Choice: Why More Is Less*, (New York: Harper Perennial, 2005). See also A. Robbins and A. Wilner, *Quarterlife Crisis: The Unique Challenges of Life in Your Twenties* (New York: Tarcher/Putnam, 2001).

6. Wilner and Singleton, *The Quarterlife Crisis: The N-Gen Transition to Adulthood*.

7. Jean Twenge, *Generation Me: Why Today's Young Americans Are More Confident, Assertive, Entitled—and More Miserable Than Ever Before* (New York: Free Press, April 2006).

8. *The American Heritage Dictionary of the English Language*, 4th edition (New York: Houghton Mifflin Company, 2004).

9. Quoted in Jeffrey Zaslow, "In Praise of Less Praise," *Wall Street Journal*, May 3, 2007.

10. As cited in Don Tapscott and Bill Gillies, "The 8 N-Gen Norms: Characteristics of a Generation," New Paradigm Learning Corporation (now nGenera), February 6, 2007.

11. Ibid.

12. Wilner and Singleton, *The Quarterlife Crisis: The N-Gen Transition to Adulthood*. Based on New Paradigm (now nGenera) Study of the N-Gen, n = 1,750 thirteen- to twenty-year-olds in the United States and Canada, 2006.

13. As quoted in ibid.

14. "Generation & Gender in the Workplace," American Business Collaboration, 2004, Families and Work Institute, http://familiesandwork.org/eproducts/genandgender.pdf.

15. The drive for additional responsibility appears to be slightly stronger in the Asia Pacific region, where 11 percent of employees are more likely to pursue jobs that provide an opportunity for promotion, compared with 8 percent in North America or 7 percent in Europe. Geraci and Chen, "Meet the Global New Generation," New Paradigm Learning Corporation (now nGenera), 2007.

16. Nadira A. Hira, "Attracting the Twenty-Something Worker," *Fortune*, May 15, 2007; "State of the Career Report 2007," BlessingWhite, 2007.

17. "State of the Career Report," BlessingWhite, 2007.

18. Geraci and Chen, "Meet the Global New Generation."

19. Deepak Ramachandran and Paul Artiuch, "Harnessing the Global N-Gen Talent Pool," New Paradigm Learning Corporation (now nGenera), July 2007; Eva Kolenko, "Parental Consent," *Fast Company*, December 2006/January 2007, www.fastcompany.com/magazine/111/next-dispatch.html.

20. Pamela Paul, "The PermaParent Trap," *Psychology Today*, September–October 2003, http://psychologytoday.com/articles/index.php?term=pto-20030902-000002&page=1.

21. "How Young People View Their Lives, Futures and Politics," Pew Research Center for the People and the Press, January 8, 2007.

22. "The $180,000 Diploma," *The Week*, May 18, 2007.

23. Beyond.com, as quoted by Garry Kranz at Workforce.com.

24. A 2006 survey by Hewitt Associates, as quoted in "Start Young, Retire Early," *CNN Money*, March 31, 2006, http://money.cnn.com/2006/03/28/pf/expert/ask_expert1/index.htm.

Chapter 4

1. Personal interview conducted by author, November 20, 2007.

2. Global numbers from *The New Employee/Employer Equation*, The Concourse Group and Age Wave, 2004; U.S. numbers from Abby Wilner and David Singleton, *The Quarterlife Crisis: The N-Gen Transition to Adulthood* (Toronto: New Paradigm Learning Corporation (now nGenera), 2007).

3. Re.sults Project EMP, *Excelling at Employee Engagement*, The Concours Group (now nGenera), 2004.

4. "The Power of Praise and Recognition," *Gallup Management Journal*, July 8, 2004, an excerpt from Tom Rath and Donald Clifton, *How Full Is Your Bucket?* (New York: Gallup Press, 2004).

5. The notion of flow was developed by Mihaly Csikszentmihalyi. See, for example, *Finding Flow: The Psychology of Engagement with Everyday Life* (New York: BasicBooks, 1997).

Chapter 5

1. *The New Employee/Employer Equation*, The Concours Group (now nGenera) and Age Wave, 2004. This research project included a nationwide survey of more than seventy-seven hundred employees conducted in June 2004 by Harris Interactive.

Chapter 6

1. Ryan Healy, "How Gen-Y is Decentralizing Corporate America," July 17, 2007, *Entrepreneurship*, employeeevolution.com.

2. Ken Dychtwald, Tamara J. Erickson, and Robert Morison, *Workforce Crisis: How to Avoid the Coming Shortage of Skills and Talent* (Boston: Harvard Business School Press, 2006).

3. Gen Y entrepreneurship discussed in Anastasia Goodstein and Mike Dover, "The Net Generation 'Dark Side': Myths and Realities of the Cohort in the Workplace and Marketplace," New Paradigm Learning Corporation (now nGenera), 2007. Self-employment discussed in Sharon Jayson, "Gen Y Makes a Mark and Their Imprint Is Entrepreneurship," *USA Today*, December 8, 2006.

4. Thomas W. Malone, *The Future of Work: How the New Order of Business Will Shape Your Organization, Your Management Style, and Your Life* (Boston: Harvard Business School Press, 2004).

5. American Express, OPEN Ages Survey, April 26, 2007.

6. Quoted in P. Ranganath Nayak and John M. Ketteringham, *Breakthroughs!* (Amsterdam and San Diego: Pfeiffer, 1994).

7. A 2002 study of the *Inc.* 500, as quoted in William D. Bygrave, "The Entrepreneurial Process," in William D. Bygrave and Andrew Zacharakis, eds., *The Portable MBA in Entrepreneurship*, 3rd edition (New York: John Wiley & Sons, 2004), 4.

8. American Express, OPEN Ages Survey.

9. Lindsey Gerdes, "Undergrads' 25 Most Wanted Employers," *BusinessWeek First Jobs,* May 11, 2007.

10. Harry J. Holzer and Robert I. Lerman, "America's Forgotten Middle-Skill Jobs," Workforce Alliance, Washington, DC, November 2007.

11. Statistics in this section from "Within Reach . . . But Out of Synch: The Possibilities and Challenges of Shaping Tomorrow's Government Workforce," Council for Excellence in Government and The Gallup Organization, December 5, 2006.

Chapter 7

1. Based on a personal interview conducted by the author on January 31, 2008, and subsequent e-mail correspondence.

2. Thanks for this observation to Martha Finney, personal conversation with author, March 2007.

3. Interview conducted by author on February 8, 2008.

4. Herminia Ibarra, *Working Identity: Unconventional Strategies for Reinventing Your Career* (Boston: Harvard Business School Press, 2003), 16.

Chapter 8

1. Unless otherwise noted, quotations in this chapter are from conversations my colleagues and I have had with Gen Y's who are in the work world

about what they like, what they don't, and what they wish they'd known before they made these choices as part of Re.sults Project YE, *Engaging Today's Young Employees*, The Concours Institute (now nGenera), 2007.

2. Rebecca Ryan, *Live First, Work Second: Getting Inside the Head of the Next Generation*, (Madison, WI: Next Generation Consulting, 2007); "Attracting the Young, College-Educated to Cities," CEOs for Cities national meeting, May 11, 2006; U.K.-based workplace consulting firm Croner, as quoted in Garry Kranz, "Employees Want Location, Location, Location," *Workforce Management*, August 7, 2007, www.workforce.com.

3. Company references in this chapter are drawn from *BusinessWeek's* "The Best Places to Launch a Career," surveys in 2006 and 2007, each based on three extensive surveys: of career services directors at U.S. colleges, the employers *BusinessWeek* identifies as the best for new graduates, and college students themselves.

4. Lynda Gratton and Tamara J. Erickson, "Eight Ways to Build Collaborative Teams," *Harvard Business Review*, November 2007: 100–109.

5. "Millennials Make their Mark," Steelcase Inc., 360Steelcase.com, 2006.

6. CollegeGrad.com.

Chapter 9

1. As quoted in Nadira A. Hira, "You Raised Them, Now Manage Them," *Fortune*, May 28, 2007, 38.

2. "The Baby Bust Hits the Job Market" *Fortune*, May 27, 1985, 122–135.

3. "Meeting the Challenges of Tomorrow's Workplace," *Chief Executive*, August–September 2002.

4. "Population Projections 2004–2050," Eurostat, press release, April 8, 2005.

5. Testimony by Edward E. Potter before the Special Committee on Aging, U.S. Senate, September 20, 2004, page 5, cited by The Employment Policy Foundation in Ken Dychtwald, Tamara J. Erickson, and Robert Morison, *Workforce Crisis: How to Avoid the Coming Shortage of Skills and Talent* (Boston: Harvard Business School Press, 2006).

6. "The Battle for Brainpower," *The Economist,* October 5, 2006, www.economist.con/surveys/displayStory.cfm?story_id=7961894.

7. "The Seventh-Annual Workplace Report: Challenges Facing the American Workplace, Summary of Findings," Employment Policy Foundation, 2002.

8. Anne Fisher, "Holding on to Global Talent," *Fortune*, October 19, 2005.

9. Robin Dunbar is "a professor of psychology at Liverpool University, correlated preference for group size with the size of the animal's brain; the larger the animal's brain, Dunbar found, the larger the size of the group. The brain limits the size of the biggest group that a human being can handle to 150" (Edward de Bono and Robert Heller, *Thinking Managers*, http://www.thinkingmanagers.com/management/management-profile.php).

10. Janet Kornblum, "Meet My 5,000 New Best Pals," *USA Today*, September 20, 2006.

11. Michael Carter, "Digital Youth Research: Kids' Informal Learning with Digital Media," as quoted in Re.sults Project YE, *Engaging Today's Young Employees: Strategies for the Millennials*, The Concours Institute (now nGenera), 2007, 8–9.

12. Lowell L. Bryan, Eric Matson, and Leigh M. Weiss, "Harnessing the Power of Informal Employee Networks," *McKinsey Quarterly* 4 (2007): 44–55.

Part III

1. Stephanie Armour, "This Is Job Recruiting?" *USA Today*, March 26, 2007.

Chapter 10

1. Bruce Stewart and Brendan Peat, "The Wiki Workplace: Leveraging Collaborative Technologies in the Enterprise," New Paradigm Learning Corporation (now nGenera), July 2007, 6.

Chapter 11

1. National Association of Colleges and Employers 2005 Job Outlook Survey, as quoted in Abby Wilner and David Singleton, *The Quarterlife Crisis: The N-Gen Transition to Adulthood* (Toronto: New Paradigm Learning Corporation, 2007).

2. Research by the American Institutes for Research, as quoted in Ben Feller, "Most College Students Are Not Literate Enough," Associated Press, January 20, 2006.

3. Based on Barbara Minto, "The Minto Pyramid Principle: Logic in Writing, Thinking, and Problem Solving," Minto International, 1996.

4. This line comes from a verse that I'm particularly fond of:
   All you needed to do was just explain;
   Reason, reason is my middle name.
   —from "Reason" by Josephine Miles

Chapter 12

1. Lyn Chamberlin, "Being Good Is Not Enough," July 9, 2007, http://www.employeeevolution.com/archives/author/thebranddame/.

2. John T. Molloy, *Dress for Success* (New York: P.H. Wyden, 1975).

3. Based on work by Chuck Westbrook, "6 Ways to Get Respect Quickly, Despite Your Youth," August 6, 2007, http://www.employeeevolution.com/archives/2007/08/06/6-ways-to-get-respect-quickly-despite-your-youth/.

4. "Within Reach . . . But Out of Synch," Gallup Organization and The Council for Excellence in Government, December 5, 2006.

5. Terry West (director of WorkSpace Futures Research at Steelcase, who was part of a group that recently studied how workers pass on their knowledge and experience, a project sponsored by the Helen Hamlyn Research Centre of the Royal College of Art, London, along with IDEO, DEGW, and Steelcase), as quoted in "Millennials Make Their Mark," Steelcase Inc., 2006.

6. Westbrook, "6 Ways to Get Respect Quickly, Despite Your Youth."

7. Based on Peter Scott-Morgan, *The Unwritten Rules of the Game: Master Them, Shatter Them, and Break Through the Barriers to Organizational Change* (New York: McGraw-Hill Companies, 1994); and "Hidden Logic Imperative," The Concours Group (now nGenera), January 1, 2005.

8. Ibid; ibid.

9. Westbrook, "6 Ways to Get Respect Quickly, Despite Your Youth."

10. Kerry Patterson et al., *Crucial Conversations: Tools for Talking When Stakes Are High* (New York: McGraw-Hill, 2002).

11. Lance Armstrong and Sally Jenkins, *It's Not About the Bike: My Journey Back to Life* (New York: Berkley Books, 2001).

index

about the author

TAMARA ERICKSON is both a respected McKinsey Award–winning author and popular and engaging storyteller. Her compelling views of the future are based on extensive research on changing demographics and employee values and, most recently, on the ways that successful organizations work. Well grounded, academically rigorous, and fundamentally optimistic, Tammy's work discerns and describes interesting trends in our future and provides actionable counsel to help organizations and individuals prepare today.

This is Tammy's second book on how individuals in specific generations can excel in today's workplace. Her first, *Retire Retirement: Career Strategies for the Boomer Generation*, was released earlier this year. The third, for Generation X, will be available next year.

Tammy (www.TammyErickson.com) has coauthored four *Harvard Business Review* articles and the book *Workforce Crisis: How to Beat the Coming Shortage of Skills and Talent*. She is an executive vice president at nGenera (www.nGenera.com), a firm offering Global 2000 companies a game-changing combination of research, education, advisory services, and software-as-a-service—packaged into category solutions and delivered on-demand.

Tammy's weekly blog "Across the Ages" is available at HBSP Online (http://discussionleader.hbsp.com/erickson/).